TRIUMPH HERALD

COLIN LINDSAY

First published 2025

Amberley Publishing
The Hill, Stroud,
Gloucestershire, GL5 4EP

www.amberley-books.com

ISBN: 978 1 3981 2161 4 (print)
ISBN: 978 1 3981 2162 1 (ebook)

British Library Cataloguing in Publication Data.
A catalogue record for this book is available from the British Library.

Typeset in 10pt on 13pt Celeste.
Origination by Amberley Publishing.
Printed in the UK.

EU GPSR Authorised Representative
Appointed EU Representative: Easy Access System Europe Oü, 16879218
Address: Mustamäe tee 50, 10621, Tallinn, Estonia
Contact Details: gpsr.requests@easproject.com, +358 40 500 3575

Contents

Acknowledgements

The author would like to acknowledge the help and assistance of those involved in the research and compilation of this book:

Mike Costigan, for his ready advice, information and excellent photographs.

Grateful thanks to Peter Truman, Danny O'Keeffe at Bradley James Classics, Rob Davies, Bryn Heeley, Clifford Heeley, Andrea Steggel, Darren Groves, David Stuursma of Moss Motors, Rich Philpott, Bernard Robinson of the TSSC and Paul Grogan for their generous supply of photographs.

Thanks to the local members of TSSC Northern Ireland for allowing me to accompany, photograph and even work on their cars over the years.

In memory of Norman Edmond, a great friend and mentor who persuaded me that I could do it all those years ago, but passed away before he could teach me everything. Still sadly missed.

Thanks to Alexander Stilwell of Amberley Publishing for suggesting the book in the first place; otherwise, like so many other things, it would have been kept 'on the long finger'.

Chapter 1

An Introduction to the Triumph Herald

The age-old saying that you cannot make a silk purse out of a sow's ear seems particularly relevant to the creation of the Triumph Herald. In the mid-1950s, Britain was still recovering financially from the effects of the Second World War, rationing had really only ended a few years before, and the general public was once more starting to explore the possibility of 'proper' motoring, so long denied through petrol rationing and wartime priorities.

The Standard Motor Company was well known in British motoring circles, through such pre-war models as the Flying Eight and Flying Ten, and in post-war years not only for the American-styled Vanguard but for the best-selling Ferguson Tractor, which used the Standard engine. The Vanguard Saloon was originally the sole model in the range, but as a forerunner of things to come was also soon available in estate and convertible form, with a sportier model following some years later. It sold relatively well, with a second model – the Ensign – added to the range in 1957, but Standard were already in financial difficulty. The Tractor Division, with it's world-famous 'little grey Fergie', was of necessity sold off to create Massey-Ferguson, and the cars, solid, no-nonsense British designs typical of the period, were already losing out to more modern, forward-looking rivals, rivals who had the financial clout to do great things.

The Standard 8 had only been introduced four years earlier, in 1953, and maintained the traditional, staid shape of things before. Other cars of the mid-1950s, the Austin A35 or the Morris Minor, all followed the rounded-off, squat and reassuringly solid jelly-mould shape so common to the British public, and Standard's latest offering was no exception. Good visibility, a spartan interior with a minimum of instrumentation, no opening bootlid – access was through the drop-down rear seat – and basic mechanicals made the car easy to drive, simple to maintain, and relatively cheap to buy, but it was basic: small, insignificant rear lights, tiny red reflectors and a hatch for the spare wheel. Realistically, though, the public wanted more than sliding windows and workmanlike interiors, and certainly no reminder of almost black-out austerity in this war-winning, forward-moving new Britain. Looking to the success story that was America, they wanted style, fins, chrome,

Standard 8 Saloon, the little car, basic but reliable, that put many drivers on the road yet still reflected the dumpy 'bathtub on wheels' design of earlier decades. (Photo: Rob Davies/A. Clifford)

bright colours, all the products of a wealthy and upward-looking economy. Yet, they needed it on a shoestring in the slowly recovering economy, where wages were still low and spare cash was hard to come by. Britain itself needed a car that would sell across the world, a car that would look to the future, not backwards, a car that would take the industry into a bright new age by shrugging off the drab restrictions of the recent past and which would sell overseas in quantity. Export was the watchword. Export – and bring back hard currency.

By 1955 Triumph were already looking at the creation of a new small car to replace the Standard Eight and Ten, and with Standard's failing fortunes, plus their somewhat dated brand name, it was decided to use the revived Triumph name. Standard had bought up Triumph in 1945, and the new brand would be forward-looking, optimistic and fresh, reflecting the approaching new decade – a car for the future.

Whilst American cars of the 1950s were becoming space age, many of the British designs of the 1950s were almost pre-war – little flair, little style, the bare minimum of chrome, just solid no-nonsense curves and panels that spoke of solidity and strength, the motoring equivalent of the 'stiff upper lip', a working car that reflected society and the sensible man in the suit or overalls. Even the colours of the time, black, grey, crimson, green, and an occasional beige, appeared almost afraid to shout out 'modernity!', and even when a brighter, two-tone colour scheme was made available for the Standard Ten, it was export only. It was a case of gradual evolution, minimal change, use the familiar and dilute the daring and, certainly, avoid spending too much money. This spendthrift, no-risk attitude was common amongst many senior management teams that amazingly still persisted throughout the British motor industry and certainly through British Leyland at least until the Austin Allegro in 1973, and reduced many a potential mechanical marvel to a dismal laughing stock. No time for frivolity, or for much innovation, which may scare off potential owners and might even be expensive to manufacture or maintain and so lose money. Like the owners, the motor car earned its keep, a solid, strong employee that would work day after day on a shoestring with little left over for frills. It's easy to be unfair to the smaller British cars of the day, which were as functional as could be at the time, but good looks, like sports cars, were for film stars or the idle rich. If you had the cash, well, the world of Jaguar or Aston Martin was your oyster, with bags of style and oodles of charm; leather and chrome luxury that shouted speed and confidence with design teams that could afford to experiment. Middle management preferred the opulence of the Rover, Riley or Wolseley. The younger, upward-moving executive went for the Triumph TR range or the Austin Healey. If you were a family man on a working man's wage you needed a good basic, no-nonsense car, or rather a good basic, no-nonsense car was all that you could aspire to, something that would justify the initial expense through reassuring reliability, and if this meant the sacrifice of expensive flamboyance on the altar of affordable tradition, well, so be it. A motorbike was for a single man, a motorbike and sidecar would suit a married man for a short time, but the family man needed a full-sized motor car and, more importantly, needed to be induced to buy your particular product as opposed to that of your competitors.

It's well known amongst Triumph enthusiasts how the Herald came about. In 1953 BMC bought up Standard's usual body supplier, Fisher & Ludlow of Castle Bromwich, and consequently were not prepared to supply components for a potential competitor in the small car market. The alternative supplier, Pressed Steel Company Ltd of Cowley, Oxford, were already working at full capacity for other manufacturers (they too would be bought up by BMC in 1965) and so the only solution for the engineers at Standard-Triumph was to have a sectional body made by a number of different, smaller manufacturers which could then be assembled by Standard-Triumph workers on their own production lines. Steel supplies were still being prioritised for the export market, and so Standard-Triumph decided to take the relatively backwards move of forgoing a monocoque bodyshell in favour of a separate chassis onto which the various sections of body could be assembled, claiming in their advertising of the day: 'Today, apart from expensive limousines, only a handful of cars share this refinement. The Triumph Herald is one.' This is often seen as a 'no-alternative' position, a fall-back to which Triumph were driven by a lack of other options, but in reality it was a clever move, not only for the designers, but for the export market, where the intention had always been to have cars assembled overseas by using the chassis itself as the jig for construction and so save money on both transportation and assembly lines.

The Mk1 Herald chassis, 'All bone and muscle' according to the advertisers. This is the early Mk1 version, clearly showing the 'stand-alone' radiator with no supporting side valences and the early rear section around the leaf spring which was revised early in production.

Of course, the generations of enthusiasts and restorers who came after would also come to bless the relatively easy disassembly and reassembly where, unlike monocoque bodyshells, any section requiring work could be removed and worked on remotely in relative comfort, without the entire car having to be rotated or the unfortunate mechanic squeezed underneath. The chassis was unusual in itself; not the well-tried and tested widely spaced ladder frame with supporting cross-members, but instead two main rails down the centre along which the drivetrain would rest, with the body overhanging each side and supported by projecting outriggers and side rails. Triumph themselves would market this as 'not the cheapest foundation, but the strongest'. There was only one problem: having a chassis and proven, reliable mechanicals taken from the earlier Standard range, what were they going to dress it with? 'All bone and muscle' claimed the advertising for the underpinnings, 'economical, reliable and durable' covered the engine, but for the outer skin, 'beautiful and functional' was the key phrase. The planners at Standard-Triumph didn't merely want a rehash of an old model. They wanted a bright, new car for a bright, new future and, even more so, needed to deflect the potential new owner from that retrograde step of a chassis underneath with the allure of what rested on top.

Time and again the designers drew, planned and threw their crumpled drawings into the bin. The vision of the future was just not coalescing on paper; there were too many limitations with the 'expected' styling and build, and each design merely repeated the traditional and tired 'bathtub on wheels'.

In 1957, Triumph's Director of Engineering, Harry Webster, took a detour from a holiday in Italy that was to change the course of the production completely. Webster was an inspiration, once Triumph's 'Apprentice of the Year', well known for experimentation and a champion of all things new, and forceful enough to have his projects considered when it counted. His style was to throw an idea into the ring, then walk away and let the designers come up with their own version, which he would then personally test and develop, often going far beyond the finished factory product. He knew that in order to take on wealthier competitors, Triumph's product had to be good.

Giovanni Michelotti, a dynamic Italian designer, was on retainer to Triumph, having already designed the TR3 two-seater sports 'Dream Car' model in 1955, and it was to him and his Turin studio that Webster turned for the body of their new project in the summer of 1957. Yet again, however, the demands of the manufacturer, and the limits of the already proposed styling, caused one frustration after another. The design just refused to metamorphose into anything other than the same boring, dated 1950s British shape. Eventually, Harry Webster could take no more and in annoyance, and in his usual style, he asked Michelotti what he would do if given free rein. The result is history. Michelotti threw away the sow's ear completely. In a relatively short space of time, he had sketched the Herald: rear fins, sloping coupé profile, two doors and forward-opening bonnet – practically as we know it today. It may have been brilliant spur-of-the-moment inspiration, or a design he'd kept in his mind until the right moment; after all, the TR3 from 1957 does bear more than a passing resemblance with large headlamps and rear fins, especially in the 'alternative' sketch, but here it was, on paper and an instant winner.

Kenneth Ullyett in his 1962 book *The Triumph Companion* (Stanley Paul & Co.) explains how the smaller drawings are then blown up to full size, and these huge drawings are then used to create a wooden framework of the full-sized car. The wooden framework is then used to create a metal jig and this in turn creates a basic car in metal, which can be fine-tuned to suit visibility, pedal placement, dashboard and boot floor, and so on.

Michelotti's original 1957 drawing for Project Zobo. (Photo: M. Costigan)

Above: The drawing becomes the wooden body buck, seen here outside Michelotti's studios in Turin, beside a 1957 TR3a. (Photo: M. Costigan)

Below: The wooden body then becomes the metal outline. The metal jigs and reinforcing are clearly visible inside. (Photo: M. Costigan)

Once complete this is again consigned to paper, and the written plans and drawings eventually instruct the production line – in the case of the Herald, three months from sketch to full-sized model, and ten months from drawing to production.

And so, a bare three months later, on Christmas Eve 1957, the first full-sized model – a coupé – arrived at the factory, with the saloon following four months later in April 1958. Large, high-set, protruding headlamps marking the front corners, tall chromed overriders framing an open, modern grille with badged cross bar similar to that of its predecessor (which never reached production) and finned rear wings that drew the eye to the aggressive chrome-trimmed tips, suggestive of aeroplane-like speed, it was the total opposite of the dumpy sturdiness that typified the Standard range up to this point, a real taste of Italian flair. Codenamed Zobo, the original intention was to call it the 'Triumph Torch' but in keeping with the Standard tradition – Flying, Pennant, Ensign, etc. – it became the Herald, which coincidentally was also the name of a yacht belonging to one of the more senior directors. Thankfully, another suggestion, that of 'Triumph Trumpet', never made it out of the starting blocks. Over the next two years the Herald was tweaked and developed, with one eye on design and the other on cost, and indeed this was a trend that was to continue throughout the Herald's lifespan, as Triumph fought to make the car affordable and competitive, but still attractive. The prototype model clearly shows the rear lamps with two chromed metal divides between the lenses, possibly for a separate tail and stop-lamp section, and a small, hooked boot handle, plus a two-colour paint scheme that may have been one step too far and

The first prototypes are then made in full size. This is a saloon, with differing rear lights and boot handle to those of the eventual production car. (Photo: M. Costigan)

so was never adopted for the road. The rear lamps, although unique to the Herald and later adopted by the Vitesse, were eventually manufactured as one-piece two-bulb units; however, the boot handle became the familiar T-shape, taken from other earlier Triumph models once again to save production costs. The major change from what had come before was that the rear lights were at the top, not the bottom. No longer the scurrying black beetle going about its business with basic illumination on drab streets, this was a car to be flaunted, as many of the colour schemes would confirm on launch.

It was not long before one of the other benefits of a separate chassis was revealed: the car came in large sections which could be interchanged as required. Bonnet, bulkhead, rear tub and, if fitted, roof gave a potential for simple restyling that was unmatched by any other car available at the time, even if this bonus had actually come about simply due to the fact that no one could manufacture entire bodies within the necessary timescale and so the sections were sourced out to smaller manufacturers. By simply replacing the rear half of the car, the Herald could be reinvented as a convertible, a van or an estate, with only slight modifications to the bodywork required and no need for expensive jigging or even, as it was all bolted together, welding. The body sections being made in different locations also kept costs low, and the whole car was simply assembled on a production line once the component parts had reached the main factory at Canley, near Coventry.

Road testing of the prototype cars continued in various locations such as Ireland or Spain, where photographs clearly show a pre-production badged front grille, sidelamp assemblies and valence design that were all later dropped. The real test, however, came in October 1958, when it was suggested that no better test for a new car could be found than an expedition that would cover the entire length of Africa, from Cape Town to Morocco. An intrepid ten-man crew set off in two prototype Heralds, already modified from earlier versions to the more familiar front profile, accompanied by a Standard Pennant Estate and an Atlas Van, loaded down with equipment and spares, to drive the entire length of Africa from South Africa to Morocco and thence across to Gibraltar and home to London. It was claimed, right from the beginning, that this expedition was not for publicity, but to test the Herald almost to destruction. Whilst full details of the trip were not revealed to the world

The great man of experiment and innovation, Harry Webster (in glasses), alongside Martin Tustin with the Herald prototype. Note the front grille with badge strip, the sidelamps and the trim around the front valence, all of which were later changed. (Kind permission of Graham Robson archives)

until after the Herald's launch – possibly to avoid the humiliation of an embarrassing failure – road conditions proved to be more gruelling and pushed the Heralds closer to the limit than any test track could ever have done. The journey certainly discovered weaknesses in the Herald's design, noticeably the cooling, which was improved before the car was finally released, and the suspension, which bounced so much off the underside of the car that every Herald ever made from that point on had a downward bend in the rear radius arms to prevent this ever happening again. The entire experience is covered in the excellent book *Turn Left at Tangiers*, and it is said that the crew was so fed up with the drive that, on reaching Europe at Gibraltar, they drove straight to London in forty-six hours without stopping, just to get it over with. Time was now running out to address any remaining shortcomings as, a bare five months later, the Herald was finally revealed

The cover of the very readable book *Turn Left for Tangier* about the Cross-African expedition on which the prototype Heralds were tested almost to destruction.

The Herald is unveiled – and assembled – then driven away before a select audience at Earls Court, London, 22 April 1959.

to the public on 22 April 1959, and in some style. Live on stage at the Royal Albert Hall, London, in front of an audience of 1,500 guests and under the watchful eye of compere Bob Monkhouse, with specially composed music and a troupe of dancers, a team of Triumph apprentices assembled a complete Herald Coupé in less than four minutes. The finished car started up on stage and drove away, thus demonstrating that everything worked (it should have, given that prior to the display it had been driven from Coventry and then disassembled again). However, the sham of putting fuel in the tank of the completed car was later exposed when it was admitted that the heater unit on the bulkhead was in fact a small supplementary petrol tank used solely for the demonstration, thus removing the potentially dangerous requirement to connect fuel lines under the car all the way from tank to engine live onstage, plus it did reduce the time needed for petrol to reach the engine and therefore prevent extended and possibly embarrassing engine cranking. The display was declared a resounding success and repeated many times in various venues throughout Europe, and the Herald itself was very well received. Gone were the drab colours of yesterday – although you could still opt for black, if you wished – and the Herald not only came in bright Signal Red (the only colour, incidentally to survive from the first cars to the last), Lichfield Green, Coffee, Monaco or Powder Blue, Targo Purple or Alpine Mauve, it was also available in two-tone, the contrasting white upper bodywork emboldening this brave new look for coupés and saloons only. Very much a child of its time, that option disappeared in the mid-1960s – although a side stripe could be added at extra cost – and was never available on the 13/60.

Unveiled in the same year as the Ford Anglia 105e and the Mini, and slightly overshadowed by both at the 1959 Earls Court Motor Show, the coupé was available first at £515 and the saloon shortly afterwards at £495, although once substantial purchase tax was

Pre-release press photographs taken at Canley for the new coupé and saloon in 1959. (Photo: M Costigan)

The new 948 Saloon at the 1959 Paris Motor Show.

added this came in at a hefty £731 and £702 respectively, even with costs cut to the bone, which amounted to two-thirds of the average UK yearly wage. It's not that the Herald was a utilitarian car, in fact, the long list of optional extras available at the time, from walnut dashboard and door cappings to leather seats, padded sun visors, fog lamps, temperature gauge or bonnet locks, show that the Herald could be very well equipped indeed, but the price had to be competitive and so these luxuries remained as owner add-ons at additional expense. The Herald was always expensive compared with contemporaneous rivals such as the Mini and Ford Anglia and so had to fight hard to justify the extra cost, even to the point of initially being released with drum brakes by Triumph, a surprising move from a company once known as 'British Disc Brake Pioneers'.

Billed as the first family car with all-round independent suspension, the rack-and-pinion steering, which gave a turning circle smaller than that of a London taxi, the amazing 93 per cent (or 13/14ths as the adverts put it) all-round 'control tower' visibility, finger-tip controls, minimal maintenance and the astonishing engine access were all hailed as selling points; the separate chassis and rear suspension less so in some circles. Some motoring journalists, in their attempts to push the car to the limits, had already found limitations with the swing-spring design, but this was often in extreme conditions, unlikely to be encountered by the average man in the street during his daily drive, and it flies in the face of a pre-release report in the Belfast newspaper *The Newsletter* (April 22 1959), which states: 'The "Herald" has roadholding of a very high order, never more impressive when the car is driven round a bend. The steering is absolutely positive.' Basil Cardew of the *Daily Express* commented in a full-page Triumph advertisement placed in motoring magazines of the time: 'Over the mountain roads and cart tracks the Herald behaved like a sports car in road-holding and sureness of steering touch' (*The Autocar*, 11 December 1959). They were mountain roads and cart tracks indeed – just prior to release, a select group of motorists had been taken to the southern tip of Ireland, in Parknasilla, Kerry, where ten Heralds sneaked into the area hidden in cattle trucks, their telltale badges taped over, were put through their paces on some of the most challenging roads in the British Isles and declared a resounding success.

The other huge bonus of the chassis construction was that cars could be despatched overseas in disassembled parts – CKD, or crated-knocked-down – and be reassembled on arrival by trained workers at their intended destination, thereby keeping transport costs lower than that of full-sized, assembled cars, a big plus point when the majority of the cars were intended for overseas sales. Depending on the destination, there would be varying degrees of local assembly, where Heralds could also be PKD (partially-knocked-down) or SKD (semi-knocked-down), and in some cases this would require the use of locally sourced components such as glass, batteries, tyres or even just nuts and bolts. In Belfast, for example, workers carried out around 500 operations, both large and small, to assemble and complete each vehicle before it could be sold. These operations were subject to close scrutiny, as was the quality of the local components used. Questions were raised about the finished standard of these outsourced Heralds reflecting on the reputation of the parent company, so in late 1959 these concerns were addressed by none other than World Champion racing driver Jack Brabham, who flew to Belfast to road test the locally assembled Clarence Engineering Heralds on the Dundrod Racing Circuit outside Lisburn. He was happy to state that he found absolutely no difference between the UK mainland-assembled Heralds, built at Canley, and those assembled by the local Ulster workforce, describing the Heralds as 'an excellent production in every way equal to a factory-assembled car' (*Belfast Newsletter*, 30 March 1960), which boded well for the intended worldwide distribution. Heralds were eventually to be assembled in diverse locations around the globe for many years with some local variations, particularly in India, and some of which, such as the Australian AMI 12/50, were allegedly unsanctioned by the parent company but showed a degree of local ingenuity to help boost sales, which would, eventually, begin to flag.

Initially, though, the all-round visibility, the amazing turning circle, and the very visible dimensions of the car, where the extremities could easily be gauged from the driver's seat by the headlamp cowls and rear fins, made it beloved of learners and driving instructors

A rare shot of early 948 bonnets being made by one of the source companies.

alike, and the Herald graces the cover of many motoring guides and learner drivers' handbooks of the period. For those of a less-fortunate persuasion, Triumph claimed that minor damage to any of the eight panels could probably be addressed without disturbing the other seven; again cleverly comparing the cheap option of bolted, easily replaceable sections with the cost and expertise of panel-beating repairs required for monocoque mishaps, and as an additional safety feature much was made of the collapsible steering column, which would telescope downwards in the event of a frontal collision and thereby avoid impaling the unfortunate driver. The ease of repair and reduced costs, through easily exchanged replacement panels, resulted in a 12.5 per cent reduction in insurance premiums for Herald owners by at least one major company. Heralds were also used by a number of police forces UK-wide, but although they were not exactly pursuit vehicles, and getting prisoners in and out of the rear seat through two doors could be problematic, they were still used widely as patrol or support vehicles.

A new model, the 948 Convertible, appeared in April 1960 for £766 2*s* 6*d* and, unlike the only other contemporary convertible, the Morris Minor, where the hood folded down above the rear seat, restricting rearward vision, the Herald's hood retracted completely into a hood well, the frame and mechanism concealed by a pop-on canvas cover. This was admittedly at the expense of the rear seat, which was considerably narrower than the saloon, with passengers losing the elbow room above the rear wheelarches, but still advertised at 37 inches wide as a 'full four-seater convertible'. This flat hoodless profile gave an uninterrupted view of the styling, accentuating the long, low look from bonnet to tail fin, broken only by the raked-back windscreen pillars, and drawing yet more favourable comparison with the American convertibles so familiar from the movies. Even though the size was almost laughable in comparison with American vehicles, and the weather often changeable, it was still a little touch of the Italian riviera on the drab streets of home, and in any case the hood could be erected in under two minutes in the event of rain. As with any of the Zobo variants, initial early photographs show a very spartan version indeed, with Standard-style sliding windows and no external door handles; the intention presumably was to gain access by sliding the window and using the interior door handle, similar to the

The convertible prototype with sliding windows, no exterior door handles and the unsightly row of poppers along the hood.

Frogeye Sprite and other small convertibles of the period. Eventually, this was dropped in favour of the external door handle, and the unsightly row of pop fasteners along the top of the windscreen was also discarded and replaced with the more upmarket internal catches.

The Herald was to prove popular; maybe not in the same league as the cult of Mini, but as a pretty, 'Swinging Sixties' car that was owned by and pictured with many famous faces of the day such as actress Diana Rigg and TV presenter Katie Boyle. John Lennon famously passed his driving test in one, although in reality he had 'borrowed' it from George Martin and is reputed to have crashed it into a concrete bollard on another date, after which he allegedly parked it with the damaged side inwards and said nothing.

Over time, as roads became faster and journeys longer, it was soon discovered that the 948-cc engine, adequate for the earlier Standard vehicles, was simply not up to the job in basic form in the Herald; this despite tweaked and modified cars having great success in the field of rallying, with high places or outright wins in, amongst others, the Alpine Rally, the Monte Carlo Rally and the RAC Tulip Rally when driven by experts such as Annie Soisbault, Geoff Mabbs or Ian 'Tiny' Lewis. This was especially laudable when many of the cars were production models and prepared solely by their private owners, who worked out by themselves how to overcome the limits and difficulties caused by the rear suspension and drum brakes. Various tuning companies also spotted the opportunity to 'tweak' the Herald's performance. Alexander provided an uprated cylinder head option including a ribbed manifold sporting twin 125CD Stromberg carburettors. Shorrock went the whole hog with a complete supercharger system at £74 10*s*, essential for the 'new motorways' and providing an additional 50 per cent more engine power and a claimed top speed of 96 mph. Sid Hurrel's SAH Accessories Company provided everything from engine tuning

The Herald went on to spectacular rally success. Here Ian 'Tiny' Lewis, Bob Halmi and Geoff Mabbs work on their cars during the 1960 Tulip Rally. (Photo: M. Costigan)

and cylinder head upgrading to manifolds and camshafts, and even wood-rimmed steering wheels – a range of speed-boosting options to suit every pocket if not every dream. It was another indication of what could have been had costs and planning permitted, and so whilst the Herald often proved more than adequate, and individual cars such as Harry Webster's personal and experimental 'Kenilworth Dragster' offered a glimpse of its capability, it was never really allowed to achieve full potential in the factory.

Modifications aside, the engine struggled, especially with steep hills, and in 1961 it was upgraded to 1,147 cc, rounded nicely and with some poetic licence to the snappier 1200. Even then output was a relatively poor 39 bhp, but still sufficiently peppy that Triumph discontinued twin carburettors, even in the 1200 Coupé, relying on uprated cylinder-head compression and camshaft to supply the extra power required for the sportier cars. The 1200 range also saw the introduction of one new model, the estate, which was a superb

The new 1200 range from 1961. This convertible has plain black interior trim, but whilst the bonnet has 'Herald' lettering it has the large, early sidelights.

An advertisement photograph for the new 1200 Estate, pitched at the family man rather than the tradesman.

workhorse boasting 45 cubic feet of rear load space, using an ingenious system for lowering the rear seat, which moved forward and downward, thereby creating an almost seamless rear platform for extended load carriage, but at £547 10*s*, plus once again the same huge purchase tax add-on of £252 3*s* 6*d*, it still came out as expensive compared with other marques. As yet, upgrades such as disc brakes, heater and screen washers were still extras, although it did feature unique heavy-duty 3.5J steel wheels. To address this price disparity, another version of the saloon was introduced at the same time: a bare-bones 948 Saloon called the Herald 'S'. Stripped to the bone and using up older but still available parts, such as the smaller engine, the initial and basic cost with purchase tax added came in at £664 2*s* 6*d*, with a sales brochure-listed top speed of 68–70 mph 'dependant on conditions'. Once the car was purchased at this basic price, almost £40 below that of the comparative standard saloon, thrifty owners could then choose from an extensive range of extras as funds permitted.

In terms of performance, Triumph also gave a hint of what the 1,147-cc engine was capable of. They were by this time marketing a small two-seater roadster, the Spitfire, which was using the same 1,147-cc engine to great effect, and so once again by changing the compression ratio of the standard Herald head, and using an uprated camshaft and manifold, they brought out the Herald 12/50, which boasted not only 51 bhp but had disc brakes and a full-length 'sunshine roof' as standard. This saloon car was unavailable in any other style and amazingly, out of over 53,000 made between 1963 and 1967, only a handful survive today. Incidentally, the advent of the Spitfire also spelt the end for the Herald Coupé, as Triumph wanted no rivals, even in their own stable, for their new sports range, and so the coupé was discontinued in 1964 following relatively poor sales, the cramped interior and restricted visibility by now appealing to neither the family man nor the sportier driver due to the 1962 introduction of the beefier Vitesse. Often viewed as the Herald's big brother, the six-cylinder four-headlamp Vitesse arrived originally in 1,600-cc guise and with the same sparse wooden dashboard and controls

COMBINATIONS

HERALD 1200 SALOON & COUPÉ
HERALD 12/50 SALOON
DUOTONE COLOUR SCHEMES

Upper and Lower Body Colour	*Centre Body Colour*	*Trim Colour*
Black	White	Matador Red
Black	Cactus	Cactus
Olive	Cactus	Cactus
Gunmetal	Wedgwood	Midnight Blue
Conifer	Cactus	Matador Red or Cactus
Jonquil	White	Black
Signal Red	White	Black
Cherry	White	Matador Red

The paint range for the Herald, all much brighter than its predecessor's.

The 'sporty' 12/50, a halfway house between the saloon and convertible, made much of the Webasto 'sunshine' roof. Most advertisements show someone standing through it!

as the smaller Herald, albeit with the single speedometer now reading up to 110 mph. The Vitesse was never marketed as a Herald variant, despite using the same style of chassis and bodywork and being a logical step forward from Harry Webster's earlier experimental Heralds. It was a model in its own right, eventually to sport a 2-litre engine and revised uprated suspension and drivetrain with more luxurious wood-trimmed interior, available in saloon and convertible form only, although a number of special coach-built estate models by Standard-Triumph at Park Royal in West London were built at considerable cost, reputed to be the equivalent in those days to the purchase price of an E-type Jaguar. Externally, aluminium bumpers and Rostyle wheel trims set off the sportier model, but it was horses for courses. Many still preferred the simpler and more sedate image of the Herald, and certainly the faster and more luxurious Vitesse with its higher price tag must have been out of reach of most of those for whom cars like the Herald were originally created.

In 1962 came the debut of a real working man's Herald, the basic and utilitarian Courier Van. Resembling the estate but with the side windows replaced by steel panels to reduce purchase tax, the Courier was a no-frills vehicle aimed at the business sector. Noisy and uncomfortable, and expensive compared with rivals, it struggled on for two years with only around 5,000 being made.

By the mid-1960s the Herald was again showing signs of age, and sales had dropped from the heyday of 1961 when 56,000 cars were sold. As a stop-gap Triumph uprated the 1200 engine to 48 bhp, with revised components including an improved engine and cooling system, but externally the rest of the car remained the same, although numerous extras now became standard fitment, reducing the profit margin still further but hopefully rekindling interest in the range. This, however, was merely to prolong the life, and sales, of the 1200 as the new kid on the block was about to emerge. In October 1967 Triumph unveiled the new 13/60 at the London Motor Show. A revised front end, using the sloping bonnet of the Vitesse but with two headlamps instead of four, covered an uprated 1,296-cc engine running a single Stromberg carburettor and capable of 61 bhp, a combination which has since been quoted as 'the engine that the Herald should have had' despite using the same gearbox and differential. Now more than capable of keeping up with modern traffic, with uprated front disc brakes for better stopping power, the interior boasted deeper, more padded seats with an even wider rear seat than the 1200, plus a revised twin-gauge dashboard system featuring, for the first time, a temperature gauge as standard, but for all its improved performance and peppiness the 13/60 was available as estate, convertible and saloon models only. No sportier model was included in the range as Triumph were promoting not only the Vitesse but their Spitfire Mk3 model and wanted no in-house competitors.

This was not, however, the end of the 1200. Even the press release information, confidentially released in advance of the 13/60 launch, stated that 'the Triumph 1200 Saloon – our best-selling model to date – will continue in production until the public tires of it and this seems a long way off yet'.

Almost all of the previous 'upgrades' were now standard in every model, making the Herald comfortable and practical if not luxurious. However, by now even the new version was fighting a gallant rearguard action against such British-built rivals as the Austin and Morris 1300 range, the Ford Cortina and the Vauxhall Victor, and facing stiff competition not only from European manufacturers such as Fiat, Volkswagen and Renault, but the emergence of the Japanese into the British market with all of their Far Eastern innovation and modern design, and, even if they did tend to rust with amazing rapidity in the British climate, the damage to sales had already begun, and Heralds were by now being manufactured at a loss.

The press-release photograph of the new revised-front and bigger-engined 13/60.

It is amazing that the Herald soldiered on as long as it did, but the marketing strategy was always based on the appeal of the unusual, by identifying this or that small, niche feature which gave the Herald an edge over cheaper competitors and therefore justified the higher price. However, as cars in general evolved so too it became harder to promote or innovate any feature which the competition had not already thought of and countered, or used and improved for themselves; eventually even the resale value was touted as a benefit, claimed as 'the most stable re-sale value of any car on the British Market'. In 1961, only two years into production, a new front-wheel-drive car was being discussed, but the amazing Herald sales that year staved off any real progress beyond the design stage, yet these figures were still not astronomical by any means. In contrast, in the previous year alone, Ford produced over 191,000 Anglias compared with just under 75,000 Heralds leaving the Standard factory – a ratio of almost three to one, the perfect illustration of what American-backed and financed companies could do, and of which the perpetually cash-strapped Standard-Triumph could only dream. By 1965 more definite plans were afoot for a replacement, even before the release of the 13/60 – remember that with the Standard Eight and Ten models before, the Herald had already been planned as far back as 1955, only two years into their production; so too with the Herald, only six years old, and here again, as before, the cost-cutters prevailed. Prototype models were still being produced, amongst them four-door Heralds and high-roofed vans, and the 1965 fastback gives some idea of what might have been, with a sloping modern rear profile, large estate-style windows and practical opening hatch. Here, the train of thought of the planners is clearly illustrated with a choice of two designs: the car was constructed with a full-sized side window extending to the line of the C-post on the passenger side, and the driver's side featured a smaller angular window, with the space behind filled with a solid panel and chromed air vent. Unfortunately, the front of the car was essentially unchanged, and thus whilst the rear half looked to the future, the 1200-style front was still firmly in the past, and so not the entirely clean break with the 1960s that the designers required for the oncoming decade. If a 13/60 hatchback was ever considered, then, like many other concepts such as the four-door Herald, it never progressed beyond the early planning stage, and the 1200 version is unique.

What might have been. The 1200 hatchback was a radical new design, in fact two designs, as the rear side windows differ on each side. Only one was ever made, and still survives. (Photo: courtesy of Car & Classic Auctions)

Faced with the same marketing and financial limitations and constraints of a decade earlier, once again Giovanni Michelotti delivered a radical new concept for the 1970s. As previously, the use of old but reliable technology and dated, trusted components to save money limited what should have been a bold new move for Triumph, and a front-wheel-drive saloon full of imagination and style turned into a disaster almost from the start. Using the Herald's 1,296-cc engine and single Stromberg carburettor, with the gearbox now underneath the engine (one reason being to attempt to retain most of the Herald's amazing turning circle), the 1300 FWD's Herald-like easily accessible mechanicals and roomy interior failed to overcome reports of poor roadholding and weak coil-spring suspension. Although once again maintenance was simple even for the home mechanic, and parts which wore out with monotonous regularity could be replaced relatively easily, buyers of the day must have been deterred by the necessity in the first place – not to mention the cost, which was considerable. Both Herald and 1300 FWD soldiered grimly on together until they were finally replaced with the 1300 and 1500 Toledo and Dolomite models in the early 1970s, which really were world-beating cars for the new decade and which had returned to the tried and tested rear-wheel-drive format and monocoque shell. The basic rear-wheel-drive and wooden dashboard Toledo was promoted especially as the car that 'Herald drivers should aspire to', but sadly was sold at a price which made it uncompetitive, not to mention unaffordable to many current Herald drivers. Amazingly, given the ultra-modern competition now seen on UK roads, which included the Bond Bug and the Range Rover, the last 1200 Herald Saloon was built in May 1970, the last 13/60 Saloon in December of the same year, and the 13/60 range petered out in 1971 with the last sales of estate and convertible models in May, by now sporting British Leyland badges on the lower front wings. The last cars endured the usual 'closing-down' indignity which all end-of-line cars face, and many were supplied using whatever parts could still be found in factory supplies. Consequently, it is not unusual to find Heralds from the last months of production that have been built using parts from the first.

Unsold stock still remained in some dealerships and it is not uncommon to hear of Heralds sold and so first registered in the UK as late as 1973, whilst overseas production lingered on for a longer period. An Indian variant was built locally from 1961, with evolved models, eventually far removed from the original UK specification, continuing on until 1983. These were all promoted and badged as Standard – Heralds having been marketed as

The eventual Herald replacement, the 1300 FWD, pictured alongside its predecessor. Although it had many unique features, it was too innovative for its own good, reputedly unreliable and never sold in quantity.

the 'Standard Herald' – and morphed into the Standard Gazel, of which by the mid to late 1960s a four-door version had been released, which allowed Indian ladies to retain their dignity without having to squeeze into the rear of a two-door car. A four-door prototype Herald was attempted in the UK, which could have assisted certain regional police forces to extricate unruly prisoners from the back seat of the patrol car that much more easily, but never made the production line. Heralds were also shipped CKD and reassembled as far afield as Australia and New Zealand – in the former they featured a unique four-headlamp coupé model called the Triumph 12/50, allegedly built using Vitesse parts as a local version without consulting Triumph UK; Malta, where they sported a distinctive cross-shaped badge on the bonnet; Italy; Belgium; Portugal; Ireland; and even in the Philippines and Peru.

The Herald also spawned a number of variants over its lifetime, helped to a large extent by the chassis, which was the perfect base for other manufacturers to add their own body design. Perhaps the most famous of these was the Bond GT, which used the chassis and bulkhead as the basis for a number of fibreglass styles. There was also the Israeli Sussita, a range of fibreglass cars which over the years used both Triumph 1147 and 1300 engines and chassis. In addition, of course, there were many kit cars including those of the Spartan and Gentry ranges, which more often than not sport MG badges, an ironic touch given the friendly rivalry between the two marques over the years and which still exists between

The Indian variant, marketed as the 'Standard Gazel', evolved way beyond the UK Herald. Seen here with four doors and a completely different front profile to the humble Herald, it continued in production until the 1980s.

Some regional police forces used Heralds as patrol 'Panda' cars, although hardly as 'pursuit' vehicles, and removing a reluctant prisoner from the rear seat may have been entertaining.

owners and clubs, even if today the MG name continues on our roads whilst the Triumph brand exists only on paper in the offices of BMW.

In total 548,291 Heralds were built (source: Graham Robson/BMIHT) and a surprising number still survive to this day, with barn finds and rare models still being discovered on a regular basis. Rising prices have turned many prospective classic owners away from the more expensive cars, and new generations are finding out just how much fun these great cars are, how easy to drive and maintain, and how simple to restore. Parts supply is excellent, and whilst many of the previously available body panels are now difficult to find, the separate chassis and bolt-on bodywork have proved much easier to maintain and repair than many rivals of the period – just as Triumph intended back in 1959. As the 1961 advertisement for the 1200 range claims: 'If you're looking for a vintage car in AD 2000, be prepared for a glut of limousines and Heralds'. Well, they were almost correct.

It is a testament to this figure of over 500,000 models that a Herald was used in the closing ceremony of the 2012 London Olympics as a quintessential part of British motoring history, and the little car has gone on to screen fame in such movies as *Paper Tiger, Too Close for Comfort, Melody* and the off-beat *Soft Top Hard Shoulder*, not forgetting, of course, television programmes such as *Man in a Suitcase, Last of the Summer Wine* and *Heartbeat*, and James May's incredible boating Herald from *Top Gear*, the only homemade amphibious car of that episode that managed to stay afloat – a fitting tribute to a car named after a yacht.

Local innovation: the Herald '12/50 Ami' was an Australian variant, using a four-headlamp Vitesse bonnet on a coupé body, allegedly never officially sanctioned by Triumph UK. (Photo: Peter Truman)

The benefits of a chassis. Some other manufacturers used the Herald's underpinnings for their own range of cars, such as this 1964 Bond GT 2+2, which also used the faster Spitfire engine. (Photo: Andrea Steggel)

Chapter 2

The Triumph Herald – A Guide to the Individual Cars

Broadly and simply speaking, there are two main versions of Herald: those with the large chrome headlamp cowls, which mark the car down as either a 948, 1200 or 12/50, and those with the slanted bonnet corners and small chrome headlamp rings, which indicate a 13/60 from 1967 onwards.

Within these two broad groups there are many variations which will help the enthusiast or potential owner recognise a particular specimen. Heralds were introduced in 1959 in two variants, the saloon with the large, angular roof, and the coupé which, as the name suggests,

The two main styles of Herald. The red 1200, sporting practically the same frontal shape as all the early cars up to 1967, sits proudly beside two 13/60s with the slanted bonnet corners and slatted grille. Bonnet aside, there is little elsewhere to distinguish either at first glance.

cut off the rear of the roof to gain a sloping, sportier profile. The convertible, which arrived shortly afterwards, is instantly recognisable, but as all three models continued for some years, being able to date and appraise a car by its features can be a bonus. It should be noted that this is by no means set in stone, as many of the modifications that became standard on later cars were originally offered as upgrades in earlier models, and there are so many options, alterations and changes over the course of the Herald's lifetime that it is almost impossible to list them all. The white rubber bumpers, for example, cannot be taken as any indication of age; they were originally absent, then an optional extra, then standard fitment, but as many reproduction valences are supplied these days with no fitting strips they are often omitted completely, due as much to cost of replacement as to any difficulty in fitting, and many have been replaced with the extruded aluminium bumpers from the more luxurious Vitesse.

All models in the Herald range used the same style of chassis, bulkhead and doors, with only minor alterations, and so visible external variations were usually the roof, or lack of it, with modifications to the rear deck, upper wings and rear tub as required, and the bonnet in later models. All Heralds have this large, forward-opening bonnet – despite the best efforts of the film industry* – which gives unparalleled access to the engine bay, with owners able to sit on the front wheel whilst performing maintenance. The bonnet may look heavy but opening is assisted by countersprings and relatively easy to lift one-handed, and whilst early cars had a central bonnet handle, this was later deleted as unnecessary. It is secured with two lower chromed latches marked with the letter 'M', many taking this to be in honour of the stylist, Michelotti, but this has never been confirmed. The early bonnet relied on downward-pointing rubber cones, which secured into catches on the bodywork, but in later cars this was reversed with the cones now pointing upward and fitting into brackets on the bonnet. The latches and cones, when properly adjusted, pull against each other, thereby keeping the bonnet panels, top and wings rigid and straight, whilst preventing noisy flex and rattles. It's interesting to note that the E-Type Jaguar, designed at roughly the same time but not available until 1961, used the same concept of forward-opening bonnet, and also sported external securing side latches but which required a special tool to open and were deleted from the cars shortly into production.

One interesting feature, although missing from very early Heralds, is the securing lever on top of the engine side valence. This swivels to meet two holes in the inner wheelarch; the outer holds the bonnet fully open to prevent wind or other forces from blowing it down on the unsuspecting mechanic or owner whilst bent over the engine bay, but the second position holds the bonnet at a lower angle, and this means that at night, for example, in the event of a roadside breakdown work can be performed on the engine but the sidelights, or headlamps, can still be seen by oncoming traffic.

The bulkhead takes in the front floorpans and the rear tub joins at the centre outrigger, just in front of the front seats, and so the same chassis and bulkhead makes up the basis of any Herald, with some alterations over the years. It is therefore common after so many years to see a wide variety of mixed and matched parts attached, and so it is essential to check the base model of the Herald that lies underneath, especially when a saloon is now a convertible,

* Publicity posters for the movie *Soft Top Hard Shoulder* featured an artist's impression of a Herald 13/60 with a rearward-opening bonnet.

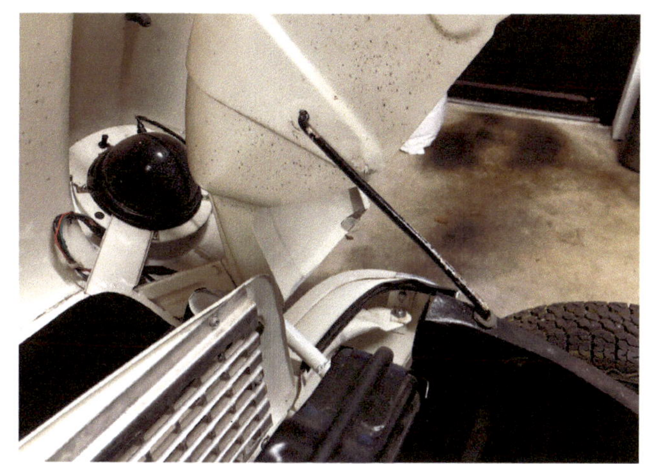

The bonnet stay, a nice safety feature, enabled the bonnet to be angled against the pull of the counterbalance springs so that in the dark the front marker lights could be seen by oncoming traffic when the bonnet was raised.

or an estate, or a Courier Van, to properly confirm a car's identity. The rectangular aluminium commission plate is attached to the side of the bulkhead, just in front of the passenger door. The long, often overpainted plate nearby is the body number. Some very original cars may have a further number stamped or welded to the front chassis outrigger; this is a factory production-line number and bears no relevance to the actual identity.

In very early cars, up to 1961, the commission plate identified the body style, and the actual commission number of the particular car. After 1961 there are usually three sections, the long top commission number being the particular car's identity. The other two sections are usually paint code and trim code.

The 948 Series

The Saloon – Suffix DL

The Herald was introduced back in 1959, firstly as a coupé and then as a saloon, both with the 948-cc engine. The saloon was the only Herald model to continue throughout the entire range from start to finish and is easily recognisable by the tall, squared-off roof with the rear pillars sporting a blue badge, which read 'Herald' in earlier cars and was later amended to 'Triumph', and the large rear window. The commission number may start with G for early saloons, or GA for the greater number of 1200s, and finally GE for the 13/60 range. Overseas export models had a GB prefix, with less common versions being GG or GH. The G, GA and GE prefixes all started at 1, with the G series running up to approximately 73571, the GA to 249873 and the GE to 83433. There were other variations and numbers allocated to overseas vehicles, but these are rare in the UK, usually having been reimported by enthusiasts.

The saloon roof was finished with a chrome trim all the way round the outer edge, which followed the contour of the rear side windows down to the top of the rear wing, with the rear roof edge and rear pillars sporting substantial chrome trims to frame the rear window. On early cars the windscreen rubber seal was plain black; this was

THE TRIUMPH herald SALOON

The original advertisement for the 948 Saloon, in Coffee and Sebring White two-tone, a colour that lasted for less than two years. No grease nipples and no heater or screen washers as standard either.

A very nice and original early 948 Saloon with bonnet handle only, and chrome trim round the grille and front roof edge but not round the windscreen. The early style of heater vent is just visible at the top edge of the bonnet. Many features were changed almost from the start of production.

reversed for later cars, which lost the front and side chromed roof trim but gained a windscreen seal with a chromed locking strip instead. The front grille aperture was also edged with a chrome trim, which was discontinued on later cars, but the grille panel itself, a body-coloured frame with aluminium inserts and a small Triumph 'shield' badge, remained the same up until the introduction of the 13/60, with the exception of the 'S' and Courier versions, which used a cheaply made flat panel. Interestingly, at first it did not form part of the bonnet but was secured in place by bolts running to the large front overriders and along the lower edge which rested on the front valence, and so remained vertical when the bonnet was raised around it. The headlamps themselves were surrounded by deep cowls of chromed Mazak, light but prone to pitting, the same material being used for the two door handles. Stainless side strips ran the length of the car, covering the wing seam along the bonnet and terminating at the same point on each rear wing just short of the fuel filler cap. On the saloon the remaining area of the rear wing was unadorned, but the coupé bore the word 'Herald' and the convertible sported crossed flags of naval design, strangely appropriate in a car named after a yacht, which represent the letters V and S – the letters V and S for Vignale and Standard, as the flags also appeared on the Vignale-styled limited edition Triumph Italia TR3 coupe from 1960, and are also seen on other collaborations such as Maserati as V and M, and on Fiat as V and F. They have also been variously claimed to display the seagoing message 'I am operating astern propulsion', possibly a reference to the rear-wheel drive, and by other not-so-pro-Herald wags as reading 'I am in distress'.

To the rear, inverted V-shaped trims both brightened and softened the point of the rear wing, as much for safety as for looks, and the chrome trims continued down both sides of the rear light unit, originally made as a one-piece trim fitting but later changed to three separate pieces. A triangular red Lucas RER24 reflector, common to other British cars and motorbikes of the period, fitted the underside of the wingtip above the large, curved rear indicator and stop-lamp unit, which is visible from both side and rear, and ends in a flat underside to complement the short rear chromed overriders rising up from below. In the

The crossed-flag badge which appeared on the rear wing of the convertible and which was finally deleted from the very last 13/60 cars.

earliest cars the large twin-hinged bootlid was in its purest form, with a simple Triumph badge above the numberplate, and even the numberplate illumination was merely a slot in the metal covered by a clear, plain lens and small metal surround, but this was changed in 1960 to a chromed Lucas light unit fixed to a protruding body-coloured metal plinth, and the bootlid itself gained 'Triumph' lettering across the rear edge.

In the engine bay all of the components were readily accessible due to the style of bonnet opening, and in early cars all units were very accessible indeed, with the radiator and engine bolted straight to the chassis. Water and road dirt ingress was soon found to be a problem, and at first the designers tried large rubber 'curtains' on the inner wheelarches, and when this was found inadequate they enlarged the metal wheelarch substantially and provided inner metal side valences along the entire length of the engine bay from bulkhead to radiator, which was now bolted directly to them and so supported up off the chassis; tags on these also supported the vulnerable wiring loom off the chassis rail and away from moisture

The bootlid of the early 948 showing the original style of Triumph badge and the very basic numberplate illumination, with the chrome trim around the roof gutter visible to the right just behind the side window.

Only a few months into production, the bootlid has changed to featured revised numberplate illumination and 'Triumph' lettering.

and damage. When the radiator was reduced in size for later 13/60 models the gap between valence and radiator was filled in with flat metal panels. The heater was an optional extra – as indeed were manually pumped screen washers – and was alternated between the Delaney Gallay unit and the later Smiths' model, with the former being more common and indeed more efficient, although both had a Lucas blower motor with single speed only.

Inside, the dashboard was originally a plain grey Portafleck fibreboard unit, made by Prestfibre of Berkshire, and unpadded on top, with short metal reinforcing plates around the setscrew mounting points. The single large speedometer, originally in Magnolia with a grey needle, was by Jaeger and read to 80 mph, and the only other gauge was fuel, incorporated into the speedometer and marked with a red reserve area. Dashboard controls – three pull cables, two switches and one ignition switch – were grouped around a central ashtray. The remaining controls, heater blower switch, indicator jewel and manual screen-wash pump, were to the right of the 16-inch steering wheel with its central horn push. Wipers were a single-speed Lucas DR3a unit, and the two screen-washer jets possessed a simple feature to prevent drain-back:

The early interior with quite a plain dashboard in reality, even if much was made of it being 'non-reflective'. Here the original cone-shaped and very rare gearknob has been replaced with a round version.

The original single Magnolia speedometer, clocked to 80 mph and with the main beam warning light in red. The fuel gauge was incorporated with a red reserve section.

a small glass ball fitted into the main body of the tube, which narrows at the bottom where the flexible hose fits. When the screen-washer pump is activated, these balls rise up into the broader area of the tube under fluid pressure and so do not affect the performance, but when pressure drops they settle down again and thereby block the washer pipe. As air cannot now enter the system the washer fluid remains near the jet and so a minimum of pumping is required to commence cleaning the screen. No powered screen washer was ever available on Heralds, although the system was improved slightly for the later 13/60 range by bringing the formerly under-dash pump onto the main part of the dashboard in front of the driver. The steering column was adjustable to suit the driver, and designed by way of a central clamp to telescope downwards in the event of a collision to prevent driver injury, and the stalks for light position and indicator were suitably long so as to be easily fingertip-accessible, emerging through pressed metal shrouds on the column. The seats of wipe-clean Vynide were also adjustable by means of fore and aft sliders, and rested on an offset rubber block of varied dimensions, which, when rotated on the seat rail to rest on any of its four sides, allowed different angles of rake and a claimed total of seventy-two different seating positions. The seat backs were rigidly fixed to the bases and unadjustable independently.

The saloon roof is attached at the front with two brackets above the windscreen, one per side to the outer edges, and secured with a bolt and a visible chromed, domed nut on top. The brackets themselves are hidden by shaped covers, which double as sun-visor supports, the other end of the sun-visor rod being secured by the rearview mirror bracket. Early sun visors were flat, unpadded, off-white vinyl-covered card, and the passenger side sun visor had a small vanity mirror attached by adhesive. A door-operated courtesy lamp, just a bare festoon bulb held between two contacts, hangs down from the top centre of the dashboard, and can also be controlled manually by means of a lever switch. The door trims and rear side trims were millboard coated in Everflex, a 'tough, easy to clean' vinyl covering.

The rear seat was relatively roomy, access through the front doors being assisted by having the seats offset on their mounting frames, higher on the outer and lower on the inner, so that as the seat was tilted forward it also angled inwards, increasing the gap between the B-post and the seat back. Due to the recessed side panels over the rear wheelarches, elbow room was good, and each side had its own revolving ashtray and

The rear seat was spacious with elbow room over the wheelarches, each passenger having a small revolving ashtray, but the front seats were thinly padded. Front seatbelts were an optional extra but in early cars attached to the top of the centre tunnel, as shown here.

cubbyhole. In early cars the rear seat could be lowered to gain access to the boot from inside, but this proved a short-lived feature. The saloon was light and airy inside, with 93 per cent all-round visibility due to the narrow pillars at the sides and rear, although the rear side windows did not open for ventilation as in some of the current Triumph range.

The gearbox tunnel took up a large part of the front interior and was pressed cardboard lined with waterproofed soundproofing, with a shaped coin tray on top, which protruded through the carpet. The gearbox itself was a four-speed box with no synchromesh on first, with the gear knob originally a conical item showing the gear positions on top behind a clear cover, but very soon replaced with a plain black unmarked globe. A long cardboard trim, painted black, ran along the underside of the dashboard as a finisher. If a radio was fitted it was attached to the lower metal dashboard-supporting rail, early cars having two brackets in place for this purpose, and a metal plate on the top of the gearbox tunnel cover provided a lower rear mounting. The factory-approved unit had a single mono speaker below the radio, but the facility was available to fit a speaker in the rear parcel shelf. The telescopic aerial was usually mounted through the bulkhead just in front of the windscreen pillar, although some cars also sported it to one side of the rear deck.

A twin-carb saloon version was available as a special option almost from the start, effectively a 'saloon-coupé' with the same coupé uprated engine and gauges, and was deemed sufficiently different from the standard model to be given the commission number GY, as opposed to being merely placed on record as a modified GA saloon.

The Coupé – Prefix Y

The coupé was also introduced in 948-cc form, using twin SU carburettors as standard and with uprated compression, camshaft and manifold. Very early coupés have smooth sides to the roof at the rear, but later cars, both 948 and 1200, used ribbed panels for additional rigidity with a side guttering that continued right down to the rear deck, the rearward visibility being somewhat less than the saloon.

A 'ribbed-roof' 948 Coupé in early Lichfield Green, with the clear differences to the rear sides of the roof, ribs and chrome guttering from the first coupés. Only one year into production, it has already gained the crossed flags to the rear wings, and the bootlid simply reads 'Herald'. The extra length of the rear deck can clearly be seen.

The bonnet handle remained but now gained a longer stainless-steel strip, which ran from the front of the handle to the bonnet nose. On each side a small badge reading 'Herald' was affixed close to the point of the rear wing, and a unique 'Coupé' badge was fitted to the right side of the bootlid adjacent to the number plate.

The 948 Coupé has three Jaeger gauges as standard, a smaller and unique white-faced 4-inch speedometer marked to 100 mph, and, although marketed as a sportier Herald, was fitted with drum brakes all round as standard. The speedometer also incorporated oil pressure, ignition and main-beam warning lamps, with the high-beam warning lamp in red, albeit a darker shade than the ignition warning jewel. Additional fuel and temperature gauges flanked the larger gauge, with the sensor for the temperature fitted into the thermostat housing and emerging vertically from it. Internal trim, such as the steering wheel, column and switchgear, was grey, with the glovebox lid and ashtray frontage in Wisteria; this colour was also used for the door-control surrounds. The dashboard is pressed, unadorned fibreboard, and the seats are a thin style usually with contrasting white piping. A rear seat was optional, and if fitted the rear squab could be dropped down to make a parcel shelf. The shape of the roof at the rear meant that rear headroom was limited, plus a longer rear deck was required compared with that of the saloon, and this area is inclined to rust over time, especially along the rubber seal, which runs the width of the rear deck between roof and body. The sides of the roof also rust through where they meet the rear wings and by the time visible bubbling is observed the damage is usually done. It should be noted that, although the coupé roof unbolts, as in the other cars in the range, the long rubber seal is difficult to source if replacement is necessary.

The Convertible – Suffix CV

The Herald 948 Convertible appeared in April 1960 at the Geneva Motor Show, sporting the same 'rust proofed and fully dust proofed' bodywork of the other models. Available first in Europe and then America, it was released to the UK in August the same year, featuring a

The very cramped rear seat of the coupé, and the restricted view from the rear window. The seat back folded down to make a bench.

twin-carb uprated engine and three-gauge layout, so is often referred to as the 'convertible coupé'. The front half of the car is exactly as the others, but here, with no visible roof, the hood frame is hinged to the B-posts, which have been restyled to accommodate the hood well behind and consequently are broader than that of the saloon, thereby limiting the rearward adjustment of the front seats despite a dimple in the metal level with the seat back. The inner wing tops differ from other models and there is an inner hood rail which follows the contours of the hood well to support the rear seat whilst allowing the hood to fold down in behind. This means that the rear-seat is necessarily narrower and thinner than the saloon, with reduced elbow room for rear seat passengers, due to the hood frame folding down on either side as well as behind, but when folded it disappears completely, leaving very uncluttered lines. Vinyl-covered flat-fronted trims hide the hood well – there are no side pockets nor ashtrays – and a shaped cover hides the hood when folded down.

A very nice 948 Convertible in Signal Red, the only colour that was available for the entire Herald range from 1959 to 1971. Here you can clearly see the chrome trim around the front grille.

The interior of the convertible was bright and airy, with piped seats and two-tone door trims. This one has an original factory radio and speaker, plus the three 'Coupé' gauges.

The convertible rear seat, narrower than the saloon and with no 'elbow' room over the wheelarches, but still billed as a full four-seater car. The hood well cover hides the hood frame.

The inner frame itself is topped by ornamental metal strips in three pieces, which finish in a complicated overlap at the B-post, originally in a white-grained coating which is prone to cracking and bubbling over time. At the front, the windscreen frame now has a welded cover over the metal seam running full length along the top, and the hood attaches by means of catches screwed into captive plates at two points along the top inner edge of the windscreen frame. Sun-visor fixings also differ from the saloon, using thinner, angled rods attached to a teardrop-shaped plate. The door, prone to opening due to body flex caused by the lack of a rigid roof, gained extra security by way of a hook and eye fixing, with the hook on the door and the eye on the B-post; even when not fitted, the two locating dimples can be seen on the B-post of most other models. The door glass also curves at the top rear corner, as opposed to the angular sharp edge of the other models, and is one of the easiest ways of spotting a converted saloon. Many Herald saloons have been converted to convertible over the years, some by simply unbolting and removing the roof, which is neither safe nor recommended, and although a more professional conversion can be performed by replacing the saloon rear tub with that of a genuine convertible, unless all of the components are swapped over then the alteration is often still obvious to the practised eye and values therefore differ from the genuine original article. In the 1960s a conversion kit was released by Tristan, which allowed the removal of a saloon roof and replacement with a hood mechanism, but for safety this uses a rather visible t-piece brace and the profile of the hood, when either up or down, is a giveaway due to the ungainly size required to cover the saloon interior and different rear deck.

Herald 'S' – Suffix SP

The Herald 'S', the bargain basement model from early 1961 to 1964, is distinguishable from other 948-cc Heralds in that there are no chrome side strips, and the front grille is a basic one-piece checkerboard panel similar to that of the Courier Van. The dashboard is grey fibreboard with no glovebox lid, but unlike the early cars that also lacked a lid, there is no

The Herald 'S'. It had a basic front grille, no side strips, no bumpers and the 948 engine, but a huge range of upgrades as funds permitted. (Photo: M. Costigan)

A press release photograph of the Herald 'S' dashboard with Magnolia speedometer and Wisteria/Grey trim. This one is very basic indeed, showing blanking grommets where heater controls and blower switch usually are.

surrounding trim either. There is a chrome strip running full length along the centre of the dashboard that was only ever used on this model or in Courier Vans, and the speedometer was the early white-faced version; the front footwell carpets are rubber mats, and there is a large chromed letter 'S' on the bootlid. The 'S' was unusual in that a twin-carb version was offered long after it was unavailable on other contemporary models; this was because it still used the 948-cc engine, but it also merited the large range of optional extras available on all the other models so, although badged as a basic model, some could theoretically have ended up with higher specification, and perform better, than the full-price saloon.

The 1200 Series

The 1200 range was released on 10 April 1961, and all commission numbers now followed the GA sequence. Cars built in the period up to October 1962 had the 'Triumph' lettering on the bonnet replaced with 'Herald', and the front sidelamp was a single-bulb Lucas L595 unit, the same L595 that was used as a reversing lamp on the E-Type Jaguar. This was more of an American affectation, where many cars had a single bulb for multiple functions at both front and rear, but it proved unpopular in Britain. It is interesting to note that a conversion plate was offered to convert earlier cars to this single-bulb look, but later, when

One of the adverts for the new 1200 range in 1961. This one now has the engine power to sport a tow bar, something the 948 would have struggled with, but has a hybrid combination of small sidelamp units and 'Triumph' lettering.

the cars reverted to the more common twin-bulb unit, yet another plate was made to enable owners of single-bulb cars to change back. The previously grey interior trim such as the steering wheel and column, and the dashboard switches, now changed to black on all cars and all Wisteria trim was also replaced in black, with the now-black speedometer reading to 90 mph and sporting a red needle, although the fuel gauge needle became white. Early in production the previously red high-beam warning lamp in the speedometer gauge was changed to blue. The seats became more thickly padded and supportive, although still without separate seatback adjustment, and the 'anti-glare' dashboard surround remained plain and uncovered until 1964; companies such as Ritmo marketed a self-adhesive padded dashboard cover as a luxury accessory. The front valence also gained a central, rectangular projection, mirroring that of the contemporary Vitesse with the lower, taller radiator, but this was for cost-cutting purposes only as the Herald never required the extra space. The Vitesse was a model in its own right, and never merely an uprated Herald, despite the common shape and shared parts.

The single sidelight and indicator unit, which had a single white bulb, was unpopular in the UK, especially in the dark where it reduced the outer lighting of the cars when indicating to turn. The factory, or dealership, would fit specially made adaptor plates to make older Heralds appear more modern, and when this did not prove a hit, they also made plinths to change small light units to large dual-bulb lamps again.

By 1961 the dashboard has changed to a single, black-faced speedometer, and the switchgear, steering column and wheel, and interior trims all became black. Controls assumed position round a central ashtray, but the wooden fascia was still an optional overdash, as shown by the recessed switches.

The bonnet handle now disappeared completely across the range, being replaced with a stainless-steel strip running the length of the bonnet and ending just short of the heater intake grille. The 1200 Heralds now sported a chromed script badge on the rear, informing onlookers of their new bigger engine, and Triumph lettering, matching that of the bonnet, was again spaced across the boot edge. In standard form the 1200 still sported drum brakes all round, disc brakes still being optional extras, as was a Walnut 'overdash', which was screwed in place over the original fibreboard dashboard, and can be identified by the recessed switches; the dashboard surround itself was still hard, pressed fibreboard but by now metal reinforcing plates had been added to the top outer corners. This was partly due to overzealous owners pulling the switchgear and cables too forcefully, which actually pulled the dashboard off the car, and the switches and cables themselves were now mounted through a large metal reinforcing panel attached to the bulkhead for additional strength and support. The dashboard controls, steering wheel, column and column switches, and window or door lever bezels and knobs were now all produced in black, and the choice of carpet became limited to charcoal grey, regardless of trim colour.

Shortly into 1200 production the chassis was revised, with thicker main rails and a revised rear section above the differential strengthening areas exposed as weak through everyday use, with the exhaust no longer emerging through the rear of the chassis. By 1963 the wooden dashboard was standard, with the switches being attached directly onto it, not merely emerging through it from the backing fibreboard, and secured by large chrome bezels; this extra rigidity from the wood removed the need for the metal reinforcing panel in behind, requiring only metal bracing strips from the dashboard under rail to the bulkhead, but the dashboard surround itself was now more luxuriously padded, attached by full-width metal reinforcing strips across the entire length of the top rear edge below the windscreen and taking in the screen demister vents. The glovebox gained not only a hinged wooden lid as standard, but also a lock as opposed to the simple spring-loaded latch of the earlier overdash.

To the rear of the car, a small '1200' badge now indicated the bigger engine size. This is an early 1200 in Primrose Yellow and White.

An early 1200 pre-production convertible, still sporting the 948 bonnet handle, used as a press-release car and featured in contemporary motoring magazine road tests of 1961. (Photo: B. Robinson.)

The 1200 Coupé – Suffix CP

The 1200 Coupé was externally the same as the earlier ribbed-roof 948-cc model, but now sported only one large gauge on the dashboard, which, despite the sportier aspirations, still read only to 90 mph, the same as the humbler saloon. By this time there was no longer a twin-carb option, and so the engine had one single Solex carburettor, with the engine itself being uprated for the extra power and speed through the usual combination of camshaft and head compression, yet it still featured drum brakes as standard. Never really being more than a two-seater Herald, it was discontinued in 1964 to remove in-house competition from the Spitfire and Vitesse ranges and only around 5,000 were made.

The Estate – Suffix SC

The 1200 Estate appeared in May 1961. This was a totally new model of Herald, there being no 948 estate, and it was an amazingly roomy load carrier, the rear cargo area carrying 19.75 cubic feet of space thanks to the extended roof area when rear-seat passengers were present. This increased to 45 cubic feet when the rear seats were folded down. Using a revised, larger 9-gallon underfloor fuel tank – for which the fuel gauge had no red reserve marking – slightly modified tub floor and a large rear door hinging upwards and supported by spring-loaded struts, it was advertised as having the roadholding and comfort of a Herald, with the advantage of the same unobstructed rear views. Twin wing mirrors were standard fitment but regardless of the interior trim choice, carpets were all charcoal grey. The spare wheel sat partially under the fuel tank, and the jack was so designed that it had a shaped 'foot', which fitted the shape of the spare wheel indent and so was stored on top of it, braced against the rear fuel-tank support. All other models had a smaller jack strapped to the side of the boot opposite the fuel tank.

The coupé continued in the 1200 range, but with a single dashboard gauge only as in the other models, a single Solex carburettor and a 1200 badge on the bootlid.

The 1200 series saw the release of the new estate. Confidential advance information was supplied to dealers so that they could appear well informed and so sell the new models to enquiring customers. Although a great workhorse, the estate was marketed at the family man with weekend hobbies as a car for both work and play, as the car was a true five-seater but with amazing load capacity.

The 12/50 – Suffix RS

The 12/50 was a unique model, having a simple silver-aluminium grille, which was fitted to no other Herald, with a short metal spear down the centre to cover the panel joint, a full-length Webasto sunroof, disc brakes as standard and tell-tale red 12/50 badges on rear wings and boot; the model also sported a red 'Triumph' badge on the rear roof pillars. An uprated engine delivered 51 bhp, the most power available anywhere in the range so far, and it proved an excellent compromise between saloon and convertible, the advertisements of the day – and many owners – making the most of the huge opening roof.

The Courier Van – Suffix V

The Courier Van was a short-lived cargo van available between 1962 and 1964. Essentially an estate body and roof with the same load-carrying capability, the side windows were replaced with metal panels, the rear load floor with bare unadorned plywood, areas of interior carpet replaced with rubber mats, and a simple square-perforated front grille. The rear door, from the estate model, uniquely had the name 'Triumph Courier' lettered across

The Herald 12/50, which featured a sportier uprated engine with a full-length 'sunshine' roof. The front grille is unique to the model, and three red 12/50 badges, along with the red rear pillar badges, indicate the uprated status.

The Courier Van was a short-lived cargo carrier, noisy and low-powered, with basic features. Although it had twin wing mirrors as standard, the grille was a simple metal pressing with no stainless side strips along the body.

it, although the original intention to call it the 'Carrier' foundered due to the name 'Karrier' already being used by a competitor. No rubber bumpers were fitted but it did have twin wing mirrors as standard, and was available in White, Wedgwood Green or Gunmetal Grey only. This was intended as a one-man delivery vehicle, with a single sun visor over the driver's side, and a metal flap on the heater – provided one was fitted! – directing heat to the driver's legs – passengers were obviously a secondary consideration. Owners found them noisy, uncomfortable and underpowered at only 43 bhp and so only around 5,000 were ever made. Commission numbers for genuine vans should end with V and as some estates have in the past been converted using left-over steel panels it is worth checking. At the time, due to lower purchase tax on the Courier, buyers would soon convert a cheaply purchased van to an estate using the latter's side windows to replace the metal panels and retrofitting a rear seat supplied by companies such as Restall.

The Amphicar

One vaguely related vehicle which may be mentioned here is the 1961 amphicar, designed by Hans Trippell in Germany. This was an amphibious vehicle, effectively a four-seater car designed to float on water and move by means of twin propellers, but instead of being the best of both worlds it was completely comfortable in neither. Although some aspects of the vehicle may look Herald-like, such as the large headlamps, the rakish rear wings and painted side-stripe, slim screen pillars and front quarterlights, the only connection was the use of the 1,147-cc engine, which amazingly delivered more horsepower in the amphicar than in the Herald. The car has in the past been claimed as an 'honorary' Triumph and appeared in many publications and at shows, but the link is tenuous at best.

In 1965 the 1200 engine received a major upgrade, changes to cylinder head cooling, the crankshaft and camshaft, with the water-pump housing now gaining two blanked-off take-off points, unused in 948 or 1200 Heralds but which were used in other sportier models, or as a dealer option, for the temperature gauge sender, which was as often fitted below the dashboard as through it. Heater, screen washers, rubber bumpers and wooden dashboard were now all standard.

The engine was now delivering 48 bhp, still less than the 12/50. Only four models continued in the range: 1200 Saloon, Estate, Convertible and the 12/50; the 'S', Coupé and Courier Van were dropped in 1964, and bar the 12/50, the remaining three were available in single colours only.

The amphicar. Although the rakish lines resemble the Herald, especially around the screen pillars, door quarterlights and rear fins, the only connection with Triumph was the use of the 1200 engine, which offered the required combination of power and weight.

The 13/60 Series

The 13/60 models, released in 1967, saw a return to three versions only: Saloon, Convertible and Estate, having major changes solely to the appearance of the front of the cars and the interior with only minor alterations elsewhere. All commission numbers are prefixed with GE and some very late engines have the prefix GK, but all had the same commission-number suffix as the 1200 series: DL, SC or CV. All models received a two-headlamp variation of the sloping-cornered Vitesse bonnet, with a minimum of chrome and a slatted horizontal grille, originally in metal but later in plastic, which now formed part of the bonnet and opened along with it. The effect of this was to make the car appear lower and so more aggressive at the front, quite apparent from the driver's seat where the front edge of the bonnet curves away more steeply than in the 1200. As with many alterations, it was cost related, and having a common bonnet between the Herald and Vitesse range could only save money against the manufacture of the 1200-style bonnet, which had been used on no other Triumph. The smaller front overriders now pointed downwards rather than upwards, being more compact as they merely needed to cover the bonnet link assemblies and not support the front grille as in the earlier cars. The central trim strip remained down the bonnet top panel, now extended right to the top edge, which necessitated the division of the air intake into two smaller sections, and the front edge of the bonnet also now sported a chrome trim strip all the way across to cover the welded seam, with solid, curved corner pieces linking to the side strips above the wing seam, which were carried over from the

The 13/60 Saloon with its revised front and uprated engine, the power and speed that the Herald always should have had.

1200 range. The wheels, still 3.5J for all but the estate, which had 4.5J, now had chrome trims as well as nave plates, but the holes around the circumference were now circular. When trims had been fitted to earlier models as an optional extra the rectangular-shaped trim of the Vitesse range was often substituted, but trims were also a popular owner upgrade, being commonly sold off the shelf in many roadside garages, and so different styles often appear that were never designed by Triumph. One other very visible change externally was the spacing of the windscreen wipers; in earlier cars they were inboard of the screen-washer jets, but in later cars, where revised mechanical components were used in common with newer Triumph models, they were moved slightly and so the passenger side wiper now emerged to the outside of the passenger-side washer jet.

The engine itself gained a smaller, neater radiator and the water pump-housing also used one of the previously blanked take-off points for the temperature sensor.

Inside, the car dashboard now had two 4-inch gauges as standard, a speedometer and matching twin fuel and temperature gauge by Smiths Instruments, and all dashboard controls bar the ignition switch and combined screen wash and wiper control were

The estate remained in the range, still a very capable load-carrier. (Photo: kind permission of Bradley James Classics)

Inside the 13/60, the dashboard was almost spartan, with two gauges and minimal switchgear. The hazard warning light switch has been added much later. (Photo: Kind permission of Bradley James Classics)

arranged in a small central recess. Although the steering wheel was the same 16-inch diameter, the light and indicator stalks now became shorter with stubbier ends, with the shrouds having changed from metal to plastic during 1200 production. The seats became more luxurious, with a different trim pattern to that of the earlier cars, and the heater now became standard equipment across the range, but all other body panels and rear tubs remained virtually unchanged bar the boot badging, which now declared Herald 13/60 in black lettering on chrome. The last of the convertible models also lost their crossed flag badges on the rear wings. A steering column lock which comprised an ignition switch was added to very late cars with the resulting slight change to the dashboard layout, which became even more sparse in appearance, as even the ashtray had moved to the top of the dashboard surround. For the very last cars a larger fuel tank, from the Vitesse range, was fitted, requiring a supporting leg, which attached to the side of the wheel well, but still retained the reserve lever assembly.

The order of these evolutions and dates of variations are by no means set in stone; there were many small changes and revisions during production, many features will have of necessity been added or removed over the passing years by owners, and it should also be noted that some of the last Heralds produced used whichever parts were readily available at the factory, and so it is still possible to view Heralds from the last years of production which were built with parts from the first years. In addition, there was often a gap,

The registration indicates this is one of the very last 1200s ever made, hardly changed from ten years earlier and still loved.

sometimes substantial, between the build date of a Herald and the date of first registration, when it was eventually sold. Some cars, particularly those which arrived at the end of one incarnation and at the start of the next, languished in showrooms for years, or were often regarded as unsaleable and so used as a runabout or courtesy car for the dealership. Thankfully, build records are available from the British Motor Industry Heritage Trust (BMIHT) and these can confirm the build date, specification and often despatch address of cars as they left the factory, a great help in identifying a particular vehicle, or determining the changes and replacements made over a car's life.

The Tristan Convertible Conversion

One more variation that deserves a mention is the Tristan Convertible. Although many Heralds are promoted by both owners and vendors today as 'convertible' by the simple expedient of unbolting the roof, this is not a safe procedure, despite the arguments of those who continue this practice and may dupe the uninitiated. With the removal of the roof a Herald loses a good part of its structural stability, and increased body shake and rattle notwithstanding, the resulting flex can cause doors to fly open on bends with calamitous results. In the event of a collision insurance companies will consider this a modification and may not cover any loss or injury. Genuine convertibles will have anti-burst door catches to prevent body flex, as well as the added body strength of the broader B-post. Tristan marketed a conversion kit, with 'Super Style' and in 'Spiffing colours', which enabled the saloon roof to be removed but the body then safely braced by using a T-bar fastened to the B-posts and screen surround. The Tristan hood is very distinguishable in profile from the factory hood, and when lowered simply rests on top of the rear deck as there is no hood well. It was a safe compromise for saloon owners and many can still be seen today, and as often happens with conversions or modifications, they have become almost as sought after by potential owners as genuine convertibles as a showpiece.

The Tristan Convertible, an add-on kit enabling the conversion of a saloon to a convertible. The large T-bar is essentail to overcome the loss of rigidity when the roof is removed, and necessitated a rather ungainly hood to cover the larger rear deck.

Chapter 3

Buying a Herald

There is no such thing as the 'right price' for a Herald. Bargains abound, as do pitfalls, there are cheap rust buckets and gleaming trophy winners, all usually priced accordingly. Buying from a dealer can mean peace of mind, but sometimes at a high price, and, correspondingly, buying privately could be fraught with danger, but can result in an honest car at an honest price. There is no hard and fast rule, and sometimes your heart really does rule your head.

A top-end price of £12,000, but worth it. You just know that this car will never let you down. (Photo: Kind permission of Bradley James Classics)

Bringing a Club member or Herald owner with you on a viewing can be a lifesaver, and in many cases it all comes down to personal preference, and ability to deal with any problems or faults that may arise. Saving money on a car which requires work is a false economy if you have to pay a mechanic or bodyworker later on, but if you can do the work yourself, it can be a substantial bargain.

Read up on the Herald, and particularly your preferred model, before viewing. MOT-exempt does not automatically mean roadworthy, and regardless of widespread practice you cannot remove the roof of a saloon and make a convertible. It may only be bolted on, but removal is dangerous and will affect any insurance claim.

Many Heralds have been modified or altered over the last sixty years, for better or worse, and many an original and untouched car should have been touched as a matter of urgency years ago, so just because it has all of the original components doesn't automatically mean they're serviceable. You may also find that a replaced component is almost impossible to

Shows always have cars for sale. Were you to make an offer on the £2,000 asking price, take into consideration the uprated engine, overdrive and Spitfire wheels. Very practical for commuting in today's traffic.

The lower end of the scale, £750. Complete, but rusty. The C-posts, doors and front of roof and bonnet all show signs of rot. The chassis is the important part and should be inspected thoroughly.

The heater intake panel is often hidden by the heater itself. On early Heralds this panel screwed on, so could be replaced.

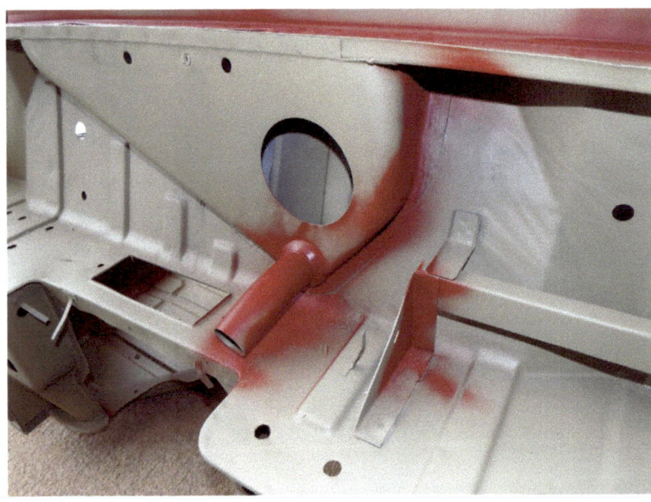

This one was restored by a master bodyworker to almost new condition, but at a price. If you can do most of the work yourself the price drops dramatically.

source, regardless of what a vendor may say, but searching for an elusive part can be as enjoyable as finding the perfect car, and if buying a rarer model make sure that any missing piece, especially if unique to the model, adjusts the asking price accordingly.

There's a model of Herald for everyone, whether the sportiness of the coupé, the roominess of the saloon, the 'hope-for-sunny-days' fun of the convertible, or the load-carrying capacity of the estate. For sedate pottering about the smaller engines are the thing, and for long-distance driving or modern commuting the 13/60 engine will cope better with modern traffic. They're all simple to work on, so three spanners and two screwdrivers will handle much of the work with nothing more complicated required. Even if you just love to polish and cosset, that chrome and shiny paint reflects the light beautifully. Be careful, though. A highly priced concours show-car may look lovely, but in reality can be a nightmare. How do you avoid paint damage in everyday use, or survive the examination of a curious public at weekend shows? Children love shiny chrome, in fact a surprising number of them will try to remove it and take it home with them under the benign gaze of loving parents. Old cars are for climbing over and playing in, every switch or handle must be pried and poked to destruction, and what can be removed or broken off certainly will be, so you will spend show afternoons in a perpetual fear of someone climbing onto your pristine bonnet rather than relaxing and enjoying the attention, and if a car must be trailered to and from shows to avoid getting dirty or increasing a low mileage, then ask yourself if that's what you want from your own Herald. It might not be everyone's cup of tea. Beware too of vendors who claim 'the numberplate has been valued and is worth ££££'. It may be, but only if removed from the car, and doing so can devalue the car itself. Sometimes, a nicely worn Herald with the emphasis on fun and driving enjoyment is the right car to go for, many of the parts required are still available, and solutions abound for almost every eventuality. A good internet help forum is often the place to start.

Once you've located your preferred car and have read up on the history of the model and know a bit of what to expect, viewing the Herald in the flesh is the next step. As with any car, try to view at the vendor's home, not a remote car park, and if you must bring cash, bring only enough for a deposit. These days, cash transfers and insurance can be arranged over the phone in minutes, and you can literally drive away once the deal is struck.

First impressions are often good. If the car looks square, or honest, it usually is. Paint should be even and although older paint may fade, a dull finish may point to a poor respray, as indeed does excess paint over rubber seals and grommets, a quick 'blow-over' to improve the exterior looks. Remember that the commission plate, on the side of the bulkhead, is merely riveted on, and replacements easily sourced to hide a true identity. Check for original

A Mk1 1200 Saloon, looking complete, but underneath way beyond saving. Thankfully, it only cost £50, but the parts have kept many other cars on the road.

paint under the bonnet or around the door apertures but be aware that many good cars have received donor doors or bonnets over the years which may still bear traces of their origins. The Herald is unique in that nearly all body sections are adjustable, so panel gaps should be ⅜ inch all round, and if the front bonnet to door gaps are large then check the fit against the bulkhead along the top edge of the bonnet. There should be the same gap here, which tells you that the bonnet can be moved back and gapped. If tight to the bulkhead, but with large gaps at the doors, then the doors are incorrectly fitted and may be suitable for forwards adjustment, but if there are good gaps at the B-post side of the doors, then the fit of the bulkhead or rear tub is suspect. Some movement is possible, as is shimming, provided the chassis underneath is accurate and sound. The work required, and your ability to get it done, should be reflected in the price. The doors should close solidly and easily, and stay closed. If they will open on a pull they'll open on corners. This is especially the case with convertibles, where the rigidity of the roof is absent, and so additional anti-burst catches are required between B-post and door. These are often missing in converted saloons, but the careful eye will spot the wider rear seat, square-cut door glass or differing profile of the windscreen surround, and know a conversion unless the conversion has been carried out safely using a convertible rear tub. It's worth mentioning twice: you CANNOT make a convertible Herald by simply unbolting the roof. Inspect the condition of rubber seals, as cracked seals will permit water ingress and rust begins very easily under wet carpets. Any area where a metal-to-metal joint has a rubber seal, such as roof to rear wings or rear deck, will also harbour moisture and by the time rust appears, it is usually from the inside out and so too late.

A door gap like this points to serious problems underneath.

These additional lower door catches are essential on convertibles, and prevent the doors flying open as the roofless body flexes.

Underneath, the chassis is the main skeleton and if anything more than surface rust is found, it will be serious, time-consuming and costly, but especially so if the main rails are perforated. They bear the brunt of water and road damage and will rust, but whilst outriggers can be replaced, there must be a solid base onto which to replace them. Rust-free main rails were once imported from warmer climes, but not recently, and are difficult to find. Water collects internally through holes in the main rails left over from the manufacturing process, or the open ends of boot outriggers; in early cars these latter were open-sided and still rusted heavily, and on later cars with the Mk2 chassis they were strengthened by being closed in as box sections, so water runs down the inside and collects in the lower areas where they connect to the main rails, or else at the dip below the rear halfshafts around the differential. This area is structural and any rust here must be cut out and replaced with solid metal. At the front the two curved front tube support arms, designed to collapse in the event of a collision, rust where they attach to the main rails, and these arms have never been remanufactured. The front cross tube also rusts through at either end, and is susceptible to accident damage. Whilst complete original tubes still sometimes appear for sale, the end sections and bonnet brackets are currently available to buy, as are the outriggers on each side from front to back, plus the two long side rails and boot outriggers. Although they can be refitted from underneath, replacing these is best done with the body removed, and it is imperative to mark the position or create a jig before removing any of the old metal in order for the body sections to refit properly, and line up to the correct gaps. It's amazing how much the body will sag with the loss of even one support. As for bodywork, the front ends, and most of the lower body, are common to nearly all the cars and so these are the parts for which repair

Hidden behind thick underseal, a chassis like this is downright dangerous and fit only for scrap.

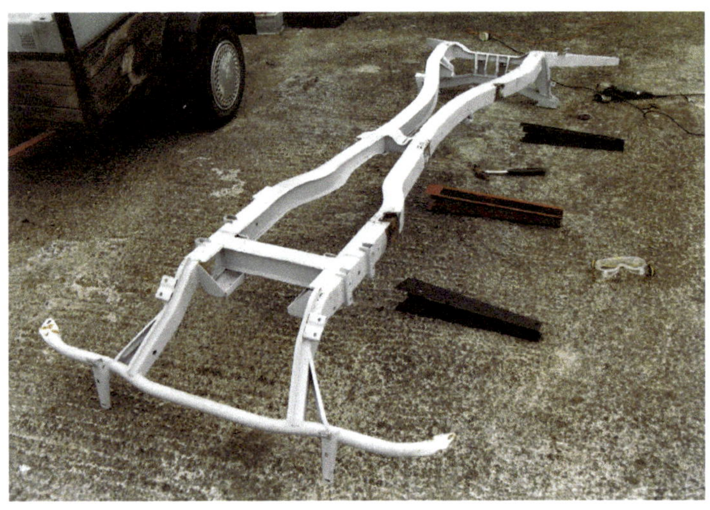
Here the main chassis rails of this Mk2 chassis are saveable, and once new outriggers are attached and positioned correctly, it can be refitted again.

sections have long been available. Lower wings, both front and rear, and wheelarches all rot, and replacement panels or repair sections are available in varying qualities and ease of fit. The important inspection is that of the metalwork behind the bolt-on panels – the side of the boot floor or the metalwork behind the front valence. Some floor sections are available as repair panels, but not all, and the long rear spring tunnel running across the car often rusts through where visible in the boot, and is all too often hidden by carpet or soundproofing. The spare wheel well also rots out along the front lower edge. Complete boot floors, functional if not particularly aesthetic, are available, as are smaller repair sections such as side closing panels or boot floor corners. On the bonnet, the area around the front sidelights rots out, as does the D-plate in behind. Repair panels for this area are available but require a competent bodyworker to create an invisible join. Underseal is also a problem; whilst it can protect a car it can also be used to hide rot, so probe any suspect areas. Some

The usual rot points of bonnet corners, lower doors and wings.

A tatty, neglected 13/60, but underneath the grime, the metalwork is surprisingly solid.

A few months later on and stripping back to solid metal and repainting has made a world of difference.

MOT testers will refuse to inspect a car that has been too heavily undersealed, as it can also hide brake and fuel lines.

To inspect the mechanical components, start with a cold engine. You can inspect components with no fear of being burnt – in all senses of the word – so look for traces of oil leaks, especially where the Herald may have been parked for longer periods but has been moved to facilitate viewing. Check the coolant for colour, either rusty brown or antifreeze blue, and watch for traces of oil on the water. Removing the oil filler will allow you to check for creamy 'mayonnaise' on the inside of the cap, a sign of potential head-gasket trouble; however this, like sooty spark plugs, may just point to periods of disuse and idling on full choke. A good drive of 10 miles or so should remove this. Check the condition of oil on the dipstick – has it been recently replaced or is it black, oily and smelling burnt? Lying down, look at the lowest points of engine, gearbox and differential for signs of oil drips. All will leak, to some extent, even just from poor parking which allows a degree of overflow, so be prepared for top-ups as part of regular servicing, but a heavy leak points to wear or damage and may require repair.

Have someone depress the clutch pedal whilst you watch the movement of the front pulley. A clear movement here points to worn thrust washers. These are easy to replace but require removal of the sump.

The engine should start up on a few turns of the starter, without prolonged cranking. The green oil warning lamp should extinguish almost immediately, with no thumping or slapping from the bottom end of the engine as the filter refills, and there should be

Getting underneath any purchase is essential. Whilst this one is very clean, a lack of oil drips may point to a lack of oil!

no smoke from the exhaust, certainly not the blue-grey of burning oil. The red ignition warning lamp may flicker at low revs, but go out completely on gentle revving.

Gear selection should be precise. A small amount of clutch chatter is often heard, as the clutch release bearing spins in contact with the clutch splines – this is normal and often disappears over time. The Herald will pull away readily, slowly in first gear but more eagerly as the gears change up, and both steering and suspension should be light and precise. A test of braking should pull the car up strongly, with rather more pressure of the brake pedal required for drum brakes than with discs, and with no pulling to either side. The handbrake should engage with few clicks, and be able to hold the car on hills as well as resisting the pull of the engine. Any bouncing of the car is due to worn springs or shock absorbers, and check the angle of the rear wheels, where acute negative camber can point to sagging springs. Wandering when driving will be worn bushes, and all are replaceable with upgrades readily available.

Exterior chromework, especially the large headlamp cowls and door handles on the earlier cars, can suffer from pitting due to the metal used – known as Mazak – and many chromers are reluctant to rechrome this material as they cannot guarantee the finish. Although attempts have been made in the past to replicate these using everything from fibreglass to brass, second-hand items or rare new old-stock units are really the only solution. All overriders and white rubber bumpers are available new.

Interior trim is all readily available, bar a few rare items such as pressed fibre dashboard surrounds and their metal reinforcing brackets, and some parts that are unique to particular models, such as convertible hood well trims or early switchgear and Wisteria trims.

Left: Once the Mazak of the headlamp cowls and door handles become pitted, it is very difficult to repair or rechrome.

Below: If the metal bodywork is sound, a tatty interior should not be a deterrent, and all trim panels are available new.

Modern soundproofing has replaced the original material, so good underlay and carpets, along with currently available trim panels in a suitable range of original colours, will transform any Herald's interior. The padded dashboard surround can be recovered by any competent upholsterer and although the rubber diaphragms of seats or sprung bases are often unobtainable, there are alternatives to retain the look and comfort of the upholstery. As long as the metalwork underneath is sound, all else is just dressing.

Always make sure of what you are buying. The author's favourite Herald receives many admiring comments, but in reality started life fifty years ago as a Royal Blue saloon. Generations of owners have made their mark, and thankfully properly, competently and safely.

The same Herald five months later, with new carpets and trims, and a home-reveneered and modified dashboard. Money well spent.

Not a Vitesse, nor even a convertible. Fifty years ago the author's car was a Royal Blue Herald Saloon. A reliable, fun car, but be sure of what you're buying!

CHAPTER 4

Maintenance and Technical

All Herald engines are essentially the same, with many upgrades and improvements through the years, with the bore increased from the original 948 cc through 1147 cc to the final incarnation of 1296cc. The bigger capacity was achieved by a process called 'Desaxé' whereby pistons were moved to one side of the block. The engine number is on the side of the block above the fuel pump and will read G for early cars, GA for mid-range and GE or GK for very late models; some variants such as GY for twin-carb engines or GB for export are less common. The HE suffix just means high compression; some export models had LE for low compression.

Early cylinder heads will have external pushrod tubes and six ports; later 13/60 units have eight ports and the pushrods are now inside the head itself. The later heads also have an uprated cooling system that has two core plugs to the rear, and a revised water-pump housing with twin ports, often blanked off.

Engines commenced at GA1 with the first major upgrade at GA80,000 when the Mk2 chassis was introduced, and the front mounting was changed from 'feet' attaching to the chassis to angled mounts on each front suspension turret. The next major upgrade was GA206641 and changes included an uprated seal for the crankshaft and revised pistons, plus an increase in power to 48 bhp.

Good 10/40 engine oil is essential, as is a good filter. Only a percentage of engine oil passes through the filter at any one time, and now that stocks of original screw-on filters are long gone, modern filters use a threaded adaptor which protrudes from the block. If this is upgraded to a larger ¾-inch 16 tpi version a better range of modern filter can be used, most importantly an anti-drain filter to prevent bearing wear during startup.

Originally the Herald had a Solex B28ZIC-2 28-mm carburettor, which effectively has a carburettor within a carburettor for cold starting. This is why many handbooks state that the accelerator must not be pressed during starting, as it disengages the cold-start system. The 1200 used the larger B30ZIC3 30-mm version, but later models changed to the B30PSE1 which uses the more common strangler/choke system for easier cold starting. All of the early models had the large air-filter box on top of the engine, with twin-carb models using a flatter oil-bath version. The 13/60 used a side-draught Stromberg CD150 carburettor, with the smaller air-filter housing mounted on the side.

The familiar 948/1200 engine with the 'frying pan' air filter on top, and the single Solex carburettor which feeds downwards into the cast-iron manifold.

The later 1300 engine now has a vertical air filter which feeds in from the side through a single CD150 Stromberg carburettor into a lighter alloy manifold with coolant heating pipe running through.

The ¾-inch oil filter adaptor which enables a greater choice of oil filter to be fitted.

Modern Ethanol fuels will attack rubber hoses and metal fuel tanks, so use of modern fuel hose and internal treatment of fuel tanks or use of fuel additives will address this. All Heralds, bar the estate, have a reserve lever on top of the fuel tank, which when moved gives access to six pints of fuel by dint of a curved pickup pipe that accesses the very bottom of the tank. Very late 13/60 models also gained a larger tank, increasing from 6.5 to 8.75 gallons, whilst the estate had a 9-gallon tank, lengthways under the rear floor, with no reserve, and even the speedometer did not have the red reserve marking of the other cars. Fuel caps for all models are a three-lug pattern, not the more common two-lug of other cars of the time.

Early Heralds, both 948 and 1200, had a wide 23-inch radiator that was narrowed for later cars and certainly for the 13/60 post-1967, the extra space being taken up by metal side panels. Both types were used throughout production in no particular order. The early radiator caps were 7 lb, rising to 13 lb as engine power increased, and the system loses water to expansion which must be topped up regularly. Whilst originally owners would swap thermostats depending on weather temperature, a good 82-degree version will suit all-year round, preferably with a 'jiggle' pin fitted to prevent air locks.

Early Heralds had an all-alloy, one-piece gearbox and bellhousing, but this was soon found to suffer stress damage, allegedly from owners of the underpowered 948 engines literally rowing the car along by the gearstick. A cast-iron gearbox body was then used, with an alloy bellhousing, but eventually the bellhousing was also changed to cast iron, presumably at a point when the engines had evolved to cope with the extra weight. First gear was such a low ratio that handbooks advocated moving off in second gear, with first used only for steep hills. Herald owners also became used to parking facing uphill, as oil would leak from the front gearbox scroll seal if pointed downhill.

The two widths of radiator fitted over the Herald's lifetime, and the metal brackets used to fill the resulting gap. Both types were used during production, but it should be noted that the top hoses for narrower radiators are longer, and cheap hoses of incorrect length will split almost immediately if stressed.

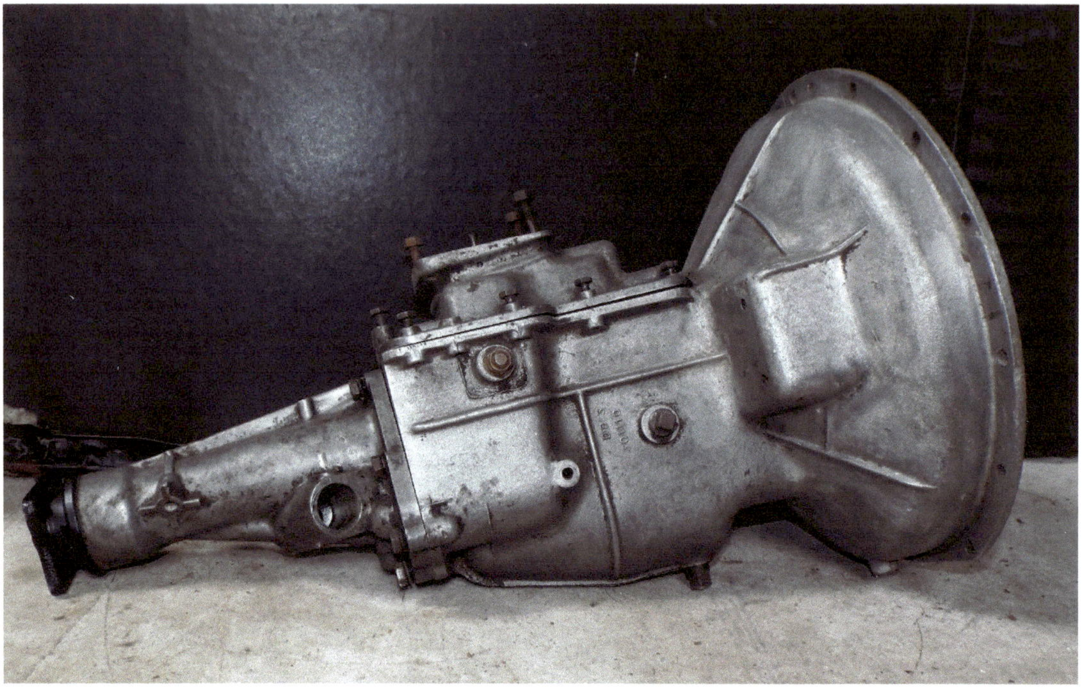

The original all-alloy gearbox, adapted from the earlier and tested Standard version.

When the aluminium gearbox was found inadequate for the job, the gearbox received a cast body, but the bellhousing remained alloy, a considerable weight saving.

Later cars received the cast-iron bellhousing, a massively heavy affair that affected performance in the lesser-powered cars, but was not subject to stress fractures.

A coil-spring clutch was fitted to the earlier cars, changed to a stronger diaphragm setup later in production. The two cannot be intermixed as flywheel and slave cylinder differ, but the later version can be retrofitted if all components are matched. The clutch release arm moves on a pivot pin which can fall out through wear, and replacements with a larger head are now available.

The rear axle is linked by a solid propshaft; although for a time 'strapdrive' versions were fitted, they proved troublesome. Universal joints on propshaft and rear halfshafts often tick if worn, and are replaceable by either sealed-for-life versions, or heavier duty items such as those from the Land Rover Freelander. Heavier circlips will also take up some wear. At the rear axle, the differential unit is a ratio of 4.11:1, although some rare versions from early cars were 4.875:1 or 4.55:1. A good EP90 oil helps both gearbox and differential run sweetly, but in the latter whining noises due to wear can be dampened by use of heavier oil such as EP140. A split pin on top of the differential helps relieve pressure build-up and should be kept moving freely.

All units will leak oil eventually through wear, and all seals are currently available, with any good manual illustrating the best method of replacement.

The electric system on a Herald is very basic. There are no fuses bar a single in-line fuse on the main-beam circuit in 13/60s. The majority of Heralds were negative earth, power

Differential oil leaks are often caused by pressure build-up. Unless this pin on the top rear mounting is kept clear and moving, oil will be forced out through the seals.

being generated from a Lucas C39 or C40 dynamo through a RB106 control box, a clever system that disconnects power on switch-off to prevent the battery from draining back through the dynamo. Early cars were non-stabilised, that is that the power generated went straight to the sensors and gauges which were then subject to the vagaries of engine revs. Some years into production a simple bi-metallic stabiliser unit was fitted which maintained a steady 10 V throughout. Stabilised and non-stabilised components such as fuel-tank senders and gauges cannot be intermixed. Non-stabilised gauges will jump immediately to the indicated position on startup; stabilised will move slowly across the face.

The braking system started off as drum brakes all round, disc brakes using the Girling Type 12 calipers being an optional extra. For this conversion, in addition to other small changes such as caliper brackets on the front uprights, a simple plastic reservoir extension was used on the master cylinder. 13/60 Heralds used the Type 14 caliper, and these will

The correctly angled master cylinders, sitting upright, with the brake disc extension tube fitted. Tilted aftermarket cylinders may spill fluid.

fit earlier cars provided the later 'chamfered' front hub is also used. It is interesting to note that the engine side valences, which had a take-off point for the longer drum brake hose, never changed throughout production, which is why all Heralds, regardless of age, have a reinforced and often obsolete hole towards the bottom of each side valence where the drum brake connection would have been. Rear brakes work on the 'leading shoe' principle where the front shoe moves, then presses backwards to move the slave cylinder along a slot which in turn moves the rear shoe. Because the handbrake pivot lever fits between the slave cylinder and the backplate, it often wears a vertical groove in the backplate which prevents the cylinder from sliding freely, and this often requires building up with weld to once again provide a smooth surface. The handbrake should be adjusted with the wheels supported, as hanging wheels will stretch the handbrake cable and give a false reading.

Suspension is coil spring front and leaf spring rear, being billed as the first British production car with all-round independent suspension. The rear suspension does have limitations at speed, where excessive positive camber led to wheels 'tucking under' and losing traction on bends, but it should be stressed that this is under extreme driving only, and many rally drivers of the day coped very well. Each model of Herald has a different rear spring, and should be replaced like for like, but a sagging rear spring can

On the rear brake backplates, this little vertical groove worn across the backplate slot by the handbrake operating lever over years of use means that the wheel cylinder can no longer slide freely, so rear brakes and handbrake lose efficiency. It will require welding and grinding back.

Here the top and bottom wishbones are clearly illustrated, the top free to pivot and the lower linked to the spring and shock absorber, which are bolted to the suspension turret.

be rejuvenated by replacing the rubber 'buttons' that fit between the leaves and are often worn away. Camber adjustment, and rear wheel alignment, is by shim insertion behind the wishbones or radius arms. The suspension pivots on rubber bushes which wear over time, giving a wandering feel, but can be replaced with uprated modern versions in varying materials and textures according to owner preference. Rear-suspension trunnions are sealed, and the grease nipple here is for the rear wheel bearings only, which unlike the front bearings require specialised equipment to remove and replace. The steering rack is also clamped to the chassis at two points, originally by alloy clamps and later by rubber bushes; again, these wear, allowing movement even beyond the famous turning circle and can be replaced with rubber or more modern versions.

The steering pivots through two brass trunnions on a threaded upright and the trunnions must be kept oiled. Grease should never be used as it cannot travel sufficiently around the threads. EP90 gear oil is recommended and should be fed in until it runs out from under the rubber cap. Very little pressure is required and removal of the grease nipple means that a syringe, or oil can, can fill the oil before the nipple or a suitable blanking plug is replaced. Trunnion failure is more common at low speeds where stress on the steering is greater, and usually at the top of the threaded section where a dropped oil level no longer reaches.

This photograph shows the downwards bend in the rear radius arm, a feature of every Herald ever made, and the bracket at the chassis, where shims are added to correct rear wheel alignment.

The vertical link then connects the top wishbone via a balljoint to the lower wishbone via a trunnion, which pivots vertically on the through-bolt and bushes, and permits the famous Herald steering.

The threads at the bottom of the vertical links are all that hold the steering on and should be sharp and clean. A lack of oil to the upper threads has caused this one to wear, and eventually fracture.

The steering column itself has a clamp, just inside the driver's footwell, that not only enables the steering to be extended or dropped to suit the driver but will telescope downwards in the event of a frontal collision. Consisting of a locknut and Allen bolt, the locknut should be loosened and the Allen bolt backed off one turn, the steering adjusted, and then the Allen bolt retightened to a point 'almost bending the lever' before the locknut is retightened fully. If in any doubt, have this set up by an experienced mechanic. The column also has two bushes, top and bottom, inside the aluminium outer tube, and these can be replaced by pushing out worn bushes then sliding new bushes down inside the tube to where they seat by means of two external buttons, visible on the outside of the tube.

Inside the car, the collapsible steering column joint is close to the bulkhead, but should only be adjusted by competent owners.

Herald wheels were all 13 inches and 3.5J, with a PCD of 3.75 inches. The recommended modern tyre size is 15580R/13. Two styles of wheel were fitted, early cars with four wide slots spaced around the centre, and on later cars these closed down to become much narrower. The colour is the cause of much debate with cars having sported silver, white or even black wheels in no particular order. All models, even the very basic cars, had chromed nave plates, with estates and later the 13/60 models having wheel trims as standard. Tyre pressures have changed over the years, with the handbook-listed pressures too low for modern tyres, but any reliable tyre-fitter can advise on suitable pressures for modern driving.

Chapter 5

Period Accessories and Modern Upgrades

During the life of the Herald many companies stepped in to exploit a perceived lack of performance from the Herald, or to improve the handling or driver comfort or convenience. In addition to the Shorrock supercharger, Alexander Engineering of Haddenham and SAH Accessories of Leighton Buzzard issued entire catalogues of improvements and upgrades. Many period accessories still come up for sale these days, although many are becoming increasingly difficult to find, especially in undamaged or complete condition, and do therefore command a premium.

For your new Herald you could have bought a rear-window venetian blind, which operated off a handle on the dashboard and protected rear-seat passengers from the sun, or prying eyes.

The venetian blind, a precursor to modern privacy glass perhaps, is operated by a turn handle under the dashboard. (Photo: R. Philpott)

Bonnet locks were also a good accessory, and still available today, although they require an almost circular hole drilled into the lower wing adjacent to the bonnet release lever. One on each side will help prevent theft or damage.

For cold weather, your radiator could be blanked off to enable the engine to reach running temperature that little bit sooner. Radiator blinds were available for the Herald by Neeta, Imperial or Jallan and were a simple, tie-on fit.

Ritmo padded dashboards were an upgrade for the earlier unpadded Herald dashboards, a little touch of luxury in self-adhesive form, and like the wooden overdash, placed around the fittings rather than under them.

The Solex carburettor was regarded as basic, so you could often replace it with more than a few alternatives. These adaptors, which bolt straight onto the original manifold, allow for the fitting of Stromberg or SU carburettors, or even a Downdraught Weber. For more serious upgrades, the twin-carburettor manifolds from the sportier Heralds were improved on by similar from SAH, Alexander or Mangoletsi, utilising Stromberg, SU or even Weber carburettors.

The Aerofan was an interesting item which pre-dated the viscous fans of later Triumphs. Spring-loaded vanes cooled the engine but as the engine revs increased, the vanes began to twist and so lowered air resistance, the concept being that the maximum air flow to the radiator was already achieved and any more was just sapping engine power.

In addition to these, there are still many upgrades and modifications that the Herald owner of today can carry out to improve the performance or comfort of their car.

Bonnet locks, which work on the release lever to prevent it being opened and the engine bay accessed by potential thieves or vandals.

warm as toast in no time!

& MAXIMUM ENGINE & HEATER EFFICIENCY AFTER FITTING

Fully up for warming up rapidly

Adjust blind when efficient running temperature is reached

Blind down in hot weather

As supplied for Standards Eight, Ten, Pennant, Vanguard and Ensign. Triumph Herald Saloon and Coupé.
A STANPART ACCESSORY.
Easily fitted behind grille.
Dashboard controlled.
Models to suit all cars and commercial vehicles.

Imperial Radiator Blind

Manufactured and supplied by :—
BROADFIELDS GARAGE & ENGINEERING Co. Ltd., Wharf Road, Ponders End, Middlesex. 'Phone HOWard 3191/2/3

The radiator blind was commonly used in cold weather to help the engine warm up more quickly and prevent overcooling in extremely cold driving conditions.

Before Triumph themselves added the luxury of a padded dashboard surround, you could buy stick-on versions for the plain pressed fibre dashboard.

Right: A selection of bolt-on carburettor adaptors fitted a range of alternative carburetors to the Solex inlet manifold for enhanced performance.

Below: Companies such as SAH manufactured alternative and performance-enhancing manifolds for the Herald. This conversion gives an 11bhp boost.

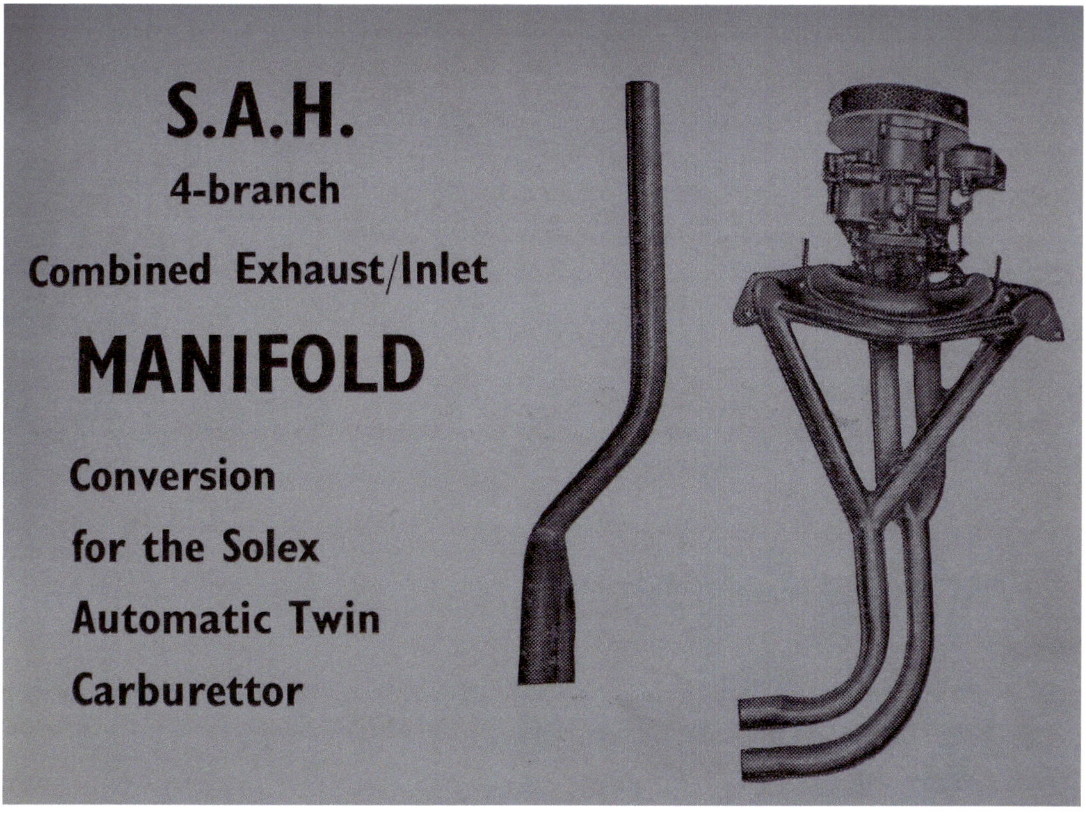

S.A.H.
4-branch
Combined Exhaust/Inlet
MANIFOLD
Conversion
for the Solex
Automatic Twin
Carburettor

The ungainly-looking Aerofan which reduced wind resistance at speed by turning the blades, thereby increasing engine power.

Alternative Engines and Components

I will merely touch on the basic upgrades, as it would take too long to detail all of the possible combinations between the small car range of Herald, Spitfire, Toledo or Dolomite. You can fit any replacement engine of the same block up to 1500 cc, as, bar the mounting points from the early engines on the Mk1 chassis, they are all the same fitment. Even the earlier engines can use the front mounting plate from the later models. The engine number on the block will tell you the origin of any engine. The small-crank 1300-cc engine is particularly sought after, and the larger 1500s have a reputation for bottom end bearing wear.

Any similar gearbox will fit, with minor changes again to clutch and possibly output flange of gearbox and corresponding flange on propshaft. Use the required clutch plate to suit the splines on the gearbox and change the flywheel if necessary.

Any of the similarly mounted differentials will fit, but this time the choice includes the six-cylinder cars such as GT6 or Vitesse in 3.27:1 or 3.89:1 ratio as well as the popular 3.63:1 unit from the later Spitfires. Be advised that better acceleration often means less top speed, and so often lower revs, such as those achieved with overdrive, are a better option for longer journeys. Some smaller engines may struggle with different differentials.

These are simple swapovers, and usually all that is required is the rerouting of cables or pipes, adaptation of the exhaust pipe (use the exchange engine's manifold and if possible, downpipe or even complete exhaust if it's substantially wider than the removed item), replacement of the output or propshaft flanges, and recalibration of the speedometer. Use as much of the replacement unit as possible, and if it's feasible use the gearbox which was fitted to the new unit, and there will be less to adapt or source. Nearly all of the mounting points are the same, bar the early Mk1 chassis engine mounts, and, if you're fitting overdrive, adaptor plates for the rear of the gearbox are also available, but this may require an alternative propshaft or having the original shortened and rebalanced. Automatic conversions have been achieved in the past but are not a simple gearbox swap. There are just too many possible combinations and variations to go into them all here, but make sure any work is carried out safely, and notify your insurance company of the modification.

Magnetic Sump Plug

A magnetic sump plug is a must-have, for both engine and gearbox. Some manufacturers make a magnetic band which fits around the oil filter, and other owners simply tape a large magnet to the outside of the oil canister. Whatever your preference, if it removes

A magnetic sump plug, seen here earning its keep.

this amount of debris, it's worth it. The Herald thread is a taper 3/8-inch NPTF thread, the 'F' standing for fuel, so that it seals with no other sealer (which may be affected by the fuel or oil) required, merely the tightening of the taper.

Alternator

No Herald was factory fitted with an alternator, but it has become a useful upgrade in these day of USB chargers, CD players and uprated headlamps. Whilst all kinds of modern alternators can be fitted, with varying complexities, the easiest option is to take an alternator which is already specified for another Triumph, for example the Spitfire, and use that. Lucas alternators such as the 15ACR were used on the later Spitfires and gave an output of around 30 amps. More common is the larger-output version fitted to the big saloons, such as the 17 ACR, which will supply around 36 amp. Some suppliers will offer identical versions that will supply up to 55 amp, but to be honest these are wasted on a road-going Herald.

An alternator is a useful upgrade, especially for uprated headlamps or modern accessories, but requires a different mounting bracket to that of the dynamo.

You will require an alternator bracket for the engine block, a spacer measuring approximately 1¾ inches, a 5-inch-long 5/16-inch bolt with suitable nut and an alternator top bracket, which again differs from that of the dynamo but is readily available. You may also need a longer fan belt, but it's advisable to wait until all is fitted, centralise the alternator in the top bracket, wind a length of string or cable around the pulleys, and measure that. A suitable fan belt of that length can then be sourced.

These alternators have internal regulators, so there is no longer any need for the control box, although if desired it can be kept in place to disguise the adapted wiring, and if the internal bobbins are removed it makes a great hiding place for a spare key. Connect the alternator to the dynamo connections, the large terminal to either of the large spade connectors, and the smaller to the smaller spade connector. Disconnect all of the wires from the control box. Connect the large brown and yellow cable to the two brown cables. Connect the thin brown-and-yellow to the thin brown-and-green cable, which will extinguish the ignition warning light. Tape off the black earth lead so that it cannot earth against anything and cause a short. That's it! If you use an old control box these connections can be hidden in behind so that all looks original from the front.

Headlamps

There are a number of aftermarket headlamp units on the market these days, offering different variations of bulb and glass pattern; in fact some such as the Clearform units have no pattern on the glass at all, but rely on the bulb reflector to safely disperse the beam. This is useful as there is no scattering of the light through the glass, so the beam ahead can be brighter. Heralds being somewhat of a minority in the classic world the choice can be limited, but in reality any vehicle that came from a modern manufacturer which used 7-inch round headlamps will have headlamp units that can be adapted for our cars. Early VW Polos, classic Minis and even Jaguar used the common units, but be careful – you will often pay more for exactly the same unit if it's marked 'Jaguar' rather than 'Mini'. These often offer a much better beam pattern that the Triumph-branded varieties, and can usually be adapted to fit, often simply by removing any of the rear lugs that do not follow the same spacing as Heralds, and if the unit has a smaller hole for a pilot light, this can be plugged with a suitably sized rubber grommet. LED bulbs are also available for every light on the Herald, both inside and out, and the rather poor performance of indicator or full-beam warning lights can be massively improved for relatively little outlay. The very bright white light emitted by some LEDs may not suit the purists, who prefer the more yellowish glow of sidelights or number-plate illumination, but LED brake light bulbs are a highly recommended improvement.

Headlamp Relay Kits

Fitting a headlamp relay means that the headlamps take on their own powered circuit, from battery to lamp, with none of the current drop through switches and the resultant overheating due to resistance. Kits are available for straight connection to the Lucas headlamp, and some have their own built-in fuses already added to the circuit. Power is taken from the battery or the alternator, and through the headlamps to earth. The original switched circuit, running via dashboard master switch and column selector switch to the relay, now carries only the bare minimum of power required to activate the relay solenoid, so there is less danger of melting the circuit on prolonged use, whilst the relay carries pure unfiltered power from battery to headlamp and so permits a brighter output from the same bulb, even where upgraded headlamp units are not fitted.

Electronic Ignition

Whilst all sorts of electronic ignition are available for Heralds, from Megajolt to Optronic, they're usually overkill. Finely tuned race cars these are not, but it's nice to have a reliable, constant spark to assist with smooth running of the engine, fuel economy and the removal of the necessity to adjust the points gap to compensate for wear. Period units such as the Sparkrite still abound which merely improve the performance of the original points, but modern, smaller module types which fit entirely inside the distributor cap and replace the points altogether are perfect, and outwardly the engine bay remains original. These are simple to fit; make sure you have bought the correct version for positive or negative

A simple electronic ignition module fits inside the distributor and replaces the moving parts of the points.

earth but it's usually for the Lucas 25D4 distributor, but this is sometimes replaced with the Lucas 45D4 distributor, so check which model you have by looking at the code, or the number, on the distributor body. Heralds used 40791A, and the code below will tell you the date of the distributor. Remove the distributor cap and pull off the rotor arm, and then unscrew the points by undoing one single screw. Slide the magnetic collar down onto the spindle, as far as it will go. If necessary, or if supplied, smear the thermal paste on the underside of the ignition module. This will fit onto the baseplate and once adjusted to the best visual curve against the magnetic collar, tighten up. The two cables go to the coil, red to coil + and black to coil - , and are usually sealed in the body of the distributor by a rubber seal. Replace the rotor arm and cap. The car should now run more sweetly but can be adjusted as per the original points setup for optimum tuning; on Heralds it's 15 degrees BTDC.

Fuse Box

Heralds only ever had one fuse, the main beam in-line fuse which juts out from the main loom in the area of the ignition coil on 13/60 models. If you've ever seen a wiring harness melt due to a short circuit, you realise just how fragile things are. A simple fuse box is easy to fit. There are many varieties, some more suited to a professional Autospark, but a simple fuse box can be fitted in a short time and will protect the basic circuits plus offer additional fused terminals for electrical accessories. Looking at the electrical circuit in the simplest form, power comes from the battery and makes its way to the various components and thence to earth. The headlamp circuit is permanently live, so that the lights can be activated with the ignition switched off, and so is the courtesy light system, which earths when doors are opened. All other circuits run through the ignition switch, so it's logical that this is an ideal place from which to take the feed to a fuse box. If you use a fuse box with one single input with a suitable number of outputs – four, six, eight or even ten – linked by a strip or buss bar, then all that is required to do is to remove the two white cables from the rear of the ignition switch and reattach them to the output terminals of the fuse box. This has already split the ignition circuit into two halves, so that even if one half blows, the other will still work. Using a suitable cable (an equivalent blue/brown wire from an old, damaged loom is perfect, but any cable of around 20–25 amp will suffice; it must be sufficiently rated to carry all the power from the battery to the numerous connected components). Connect the terminal on the ignition switch from which the white cables were removed to the input on the fuse box. You can experiment with modern blade fuses to obtain the correct rating; 20 amp on these main circuits is fine, but as the original glass fuses for period Triumphs are rated 17 amp, 15 amp would probably suffice. Other accessories, such as the heater blower, overdrive or radio, can be attached to the spare fuse box terminals using smaller, for example 5-amp, fuses. These circuits will only work when the ignition key is turned to the 'on' position, so there is no danger of leaving anything switched on and flattening the battery, and if you do have something like an alarm that must be continuously powered, then power can be taken from the other spare terminals on the ignition switch. If a circuit shorts out the damage is then limited, and some fuse boxes have an LED to indicate which fuse has failed.

Voltmeter/Oil Pressure/Rev Counter

With the exception of the earlier coupé models Heralds had a sparsity of gauges: speedometer and fuel, maybe temperature depending on the model or as an optional extra. It's nice to be able to add additional gauges such as a tachometer, oil pressure gauge or voltmeter but beware, they don't call them worry gauges for nothing. Most are very easily fitted, requiring a minimum of work or expertise, and the only real concern is where exactly to fit them. The Herald, with its wooden dashboard, allows for a variety of placements, as it's really only the other components or space in behind that limit the setting, and you can elect to have extra gauges as pods on top of the dash, in suitable brackets beneath or else fitted into the dash itself. In some cars, such as the 13/60, there is ample free space on the plain wooden facia.

If you shop around, there are plenty of period gauges for sale, and many new with a 'retro' look, but make sure they blend in with your existing array. A modern gauge with bright-blue LED lighting may spoil the mood generated at night by your existing pale-green Smiths bulbs.

A vacuum gauge, often called an Econometer, uses a take-off from the manifold to highlight fuel consumption. Keeping the needle in the green helps improve mileage. It requires a take-off, drilled and tapped into the manifold with a flexible air hose running to

The wooden dashboard of the Herald lends itself to much modification. Extra gauges are very easily fitted and the only limit is the owner's imagination.

the rear of the gauge, and usually a light source, which can be piggybacked off the red and white wiring of the existing gauge light circuit.

A voltmeter shows the state of charge, and is much more easily fitted than an ammeter, which indicates the actual current usage and so requires heavy-duty cable and connections into the electrical circuit. The Smiths 'battery condition' gauge is a nice little voltmeter and requires only power in, for example from a spare take-off on the ignition switch, and an earth connection. This will tell you more than the little red ignition warning light, the equivalent of 'how much?' compared with 'yes/no?'.

An oil pressure gauge will give an indication of the oil pump output and how this circles through the engine; worn bearings allowing oil to easily bypass other major components, or just low oil level, will show as a drop in pressure compared with the engine 'norm' and the engine will become starved of oil, leading to increased wear and visible smoke, which is an MOT fail. This requires a take-off from the oil pressure switch outlet, usually a tapered t-piece fitting that seals as it is tightened, with an oil pipe to the gauge on one end and the original oil pressure switch refitted to the other, to extinguish the green oil pressure warning light. You will soon recognise good oil pressure that can drop alarmingly – but normally – on idle, when hot, and any deviation will soon become apparent before it becomes harmful to the engine. The factory oil pressure figure was 60 lb sq. at 2,000 rpm, so any drop from this during normal use will indicate a problem.

A tachometer – NOT a rev counter – helps you recognise excessively high revs and when to change gear and so allows for smooth performance, enhancing engine and clutch life, and fuel consumption. The more common term 'rev counter' refers to a device that counts the total number of revolutions of an engine, usually industrial or agricultural, in order to determine wear or service intervals. Tachometers were available in different models of Triumph, so these will be a straight connection for the Herald, if not a straight fit due to the size; they were all 4-inch diameter. Smaller 2- or 3-inch models appear for sale all the time, both period and modern, so it comes down to personal preference. All they require, apart from illumination, is power in, earth out and an activation, usually just a connection to the negative terminal of the coil.

Overdrive

Overdrive was never an option on factory-spec Heralds, although it is rumoured that one or two were fitted at owner's request, usually the D-type Laycock de Normanville unit. The D-type is power-hungry, requiring a relay to channel the extra electrical power to the solenoid. For a simple, non-standard but very easily fitted overdrive, the J-type from a Spitfire 1300 can be used, but you require the complete gearbox and overdrive unit. Simply attaching an overdrive to the rear of an existing gearbox is difficult and requires serious work. The J-type, never available on Heralds, uses less power so does not require intricate electric wiring, just power in and out, and is also rated at 25 per cent reduction in engine revs. The three-rail gearbox – NOT single rail – is a straight fit to the bellhousing, using a clutch plate from the Spitfire in order to suit the splines on the input shaft. The rear of the overdrive unit sits slightly further to the rear, so requires an extension to the gearbox mount which is readily available. The extra length also means that a shorter propshaft is required

A J-type overdrive gearbox from a Spitfire 1300 is an almost straight replacement, and drops the revs at speed by around 25 per cent to give a relaxed drive.

but the good news is that a non-overdrive Vitesse propshaft fits with no modification, so there is no need for shortening and rebalancing. Using the existing hydraulics and a small angle-drive for the speedometer cable (which now enters parallel to the gearbox, not at right angles), all that is required is an electrical connection. The overdrive will only work in third and fourth gears, due to an inhibitor switch on the gearbox, and requires an on-off switch, which can be column-mounted, gearknob-mounted or placed anywhere within easy reach of the driver. The simple electrical circuit supplies power to the switch, from there to the inhibitor, thence to the solenoid, and from there to earth with simple in/out connections each time. The one downside is the price of the solenoid, approximately £30 for D-type but a hefty £120 or more for J-type. A simple flick of the switch in fourth sees the revs dropping from 3,500 rpm to just around 2,700 rpm and is an excellent cruising aid on long, smooth journeys where the engine remains at constant speed and there is no change in load for prolonged periods.

Uprated Seatbelts

Originally Heralds had no seatbelts at all. When three-point seatbelts were fitted, fitting points are centre tunnel, floor beside B-post, and inner rear wings for saloon and estate. Convertibles must use a two-point top fitting at the B-post otherwise the reduced metalwork here may not be sufficient to hold in the event of a collision. In the centre, early cars have a reinforced plate on top of the propshaft tunnel into which the belt brackets screw, and later cars have a stronger setup with threaded eyebolts screwing through the body into the

If fitting seatbelts, they attach to the inside of the rear-wing top rail on all models bar the convertible, where they bolt at two points into the B-post structure; anything less is too weak to hold in the event of a collision.

actual chassis. The lower outer point originally had a hooped fitting through the floor into a small reinforcing plate, but this later changed to a reinforced screw point along the floorpan side. 13/60 convertibles had static belts which attached to the rear wheelarch and emerged through the side trims at the rear seat. If fitting retractable seatbelts, a suitable version must be selected that permits the reel to mount at an angle away from vertical, and that does not foul the hood mechanism in convertibles.

Uprated Seats

Many modern seats from modern cars will fit, although all require some modification in the form of under-seat brackets to suit the Herald floorpan. Mazda MX5 seats are a common replacement, especially in convertibles, where they will fit the narrower interior and clear the broader B-post; there are a number of online guides to fitting readily available. The taller back of many modern seats, or fitted headrests, also provides better safety in the event of a collision, but width and leg clearance against the steering wheel can be an issue.

Fuel

With Ethanol-proof fuel pipes only the rubber parts require changing, which on the 948 and 1200 is the small flexible pipe from the top of the fuel tank to the metal pipe only, and on

Almost an essential must-have, a good fuel filter will prevent many breakdowns.

13/60s the additional small pipe which connects the fuel line to the Stromberg carburettor. A good fuel filter is also recommended, although not the glass versions, which can shatter, but the plastic models that can be replaced cheaply as a service item. Fitted between main fuel line and pump, or between pump and carburettor, they'll help prevent rust flakes from the tank getting to the carb, especially if the reserve is used in an emergency.

Uprated Suspension Bushes

Uprated bushes, to replace the worn and wandery rubber originals, are available in a range of textures to suit driver requirements, for more direct steering and greater roadholding. The key is striking a balance between teeth-juddering road vibration and directness of steering and suspension. Different manufacturers use differing colours, so the colour is no guide to hardness, but a good set is easily fitted and transforms the drive, and similarly for uprated steering bushes.

Uprated suspension bushes, like these top wishbone bushes, transform the handling of the car. They are simple to fit and are available in a range of materials to suit the preferred drive style.

Upgraded steering bushes have less vibration than alloy mounts and less movement than rubber originals.

What You Don't Need

- Drilled or grooved discs. These are not required at all on a standard Herald, unless you drive very fast, stand on the brakes at every junction and want pads to wear out with alarming frequency. 'Fast Road Use' usually doesn't apply to Heralds. Four-pot brake calipers are also overkill whilst some hardened brake pads never bed-in properly under normal driving conditions, but for improved performance Mintex 1144 pads are highly recommended.
- Adjustable shock absorbers. Possibly required, if your current versions are worn out and you have doubts about the quality of currently available standard replacements. Spending hundreds of pounds on adjustable gas-filled shock absorbers makes no sense if your car regularly drives under 50 mph and you don't need to worry about stability on extreme cornering, so all they're really useful for is to adjust the mean-looking stance of your car when parked.
- Oil cooler. This is not required unless your highly tuned engine is used for racing. If you must fit one, buy an in-line thermostat too, which will demonstrate to you why it never achieves sufficient temperature to allow the oil into the cooler. Additionally, a rocker assembly oil take-off kit which runs an oil pipe from the rear of the cylinder head will starve the rest of the engine of necessary oil.
- Hardened valve seats. Install these only when required, which may be never. It takes many miles for a Herald engine to wear the standard seats, which will have been cushioned by lead over the first three decades of life, and this lead memory does take time to wear away, especially with limited mileage and weekend use only. Using a lead-additive and octane booster will restore some of the performance and help prevent speedy wear, and so you can monitor your engine carefully and replace the seats, or the head as a complete unit, only when really necessary.

Essential Reading

Unlike my previous Triumphs, by the time I obtained my first Herald in 1993, I had the benefit of some excellent reference books to assist me.

First and foremost of these was the John Kipping catalogue, which was my bible of the day and of which tattered copies still come up for sale, and along with the worthy runner-up, the Rimmer Brothers' catalogue, contained fully explained, exploded diagrams and showed me what parts or units should look like, where they should go and what held them in place. I'd recommend a copy of either of these to any prospective Herald owner.

Secondly but not secondary in any way I must thank Mike Costigan and his excellent book which I bought back in 1993. *Complete Guide to Triumph Herald and Vitesse,* published by Bay View Books, is a superb reference book and one which has refreshed my memory many times over the compilation of this book. In addition, Mike himself has been a mine of information and supplied excellent copies of many of the early development or press photos used here, and I cannot thank him enough for his willingness to assist.

If you can, find a copy of the original *Owner's Repair Manual* from the Standard-Triumph Service Division, part number 508912. This is a detailed manual, published in the early 1960s, and so has the original – and best – data on these cars and how to maintain them. A good workshop manual is also a bonus, especially if you can locate the six-part series again issued by Triumph's Service Division which I find easier to follow than the large single-volume Vitesse/Spitfire/Herald version. Harder to find are the Service Training Notes issued to Triumph workers and dealerships. Featuring a range of topics, these are straightforward notes, intended to be used in conjunction with a film strip, for the instruction of mechanics in training classes.

The AA's *Book of the Car* is surprisingly relevant, with many of the reference photographs being of a Triumph Vitesse. Aimed at the amateur mechanic, everything is explained with great clarity and is a good starting point for anyone new to classic cars.

Another good buy from the 1990s is Lindsay Porter and Peter William's *Guide to Purchase and DIY Restoration* where a picture certainly is worth a thousand words, and there are plenty of them.

For more manageable-sized books, a rare but good find is Peter Russek's *Triumph Herald Repair Guide,* a mine of very clear and concise data and how-tos. Period books on the

Herald by Pitman, Hartley, Olysager and Postlethwaite also come up for sale regularly. The Haynes Manual is a source I've referred to many times in my garage, and similarly styled books such as the Autodata, Autobook, Inter-europe or Handybook series are an interesting alternative when you need a second opinion in the garage, or a slightly different illustration.

For more in-depth reading on the development of the Herald I can recommend the late and sorely missed Graham Robson's *Triumph Herald and Vitesse – The Complete Story*, his earlier collaboration with Richard Langworth, *Triumph Cars*, and Kenneth Ullyett's *The Triumph Companion*.

For those with sporting preferences, *Tuning Standard Triumphs* by R. Hudson-Evans or G. Thomas' *Tuning Manual for Standard Triumph Cars produced between 1959 and 1980* are good finds.

As a local Northern Ireland angle, a copy of Paul Robinson's *Clarence Engineering Co. Ltd* was essential reading and supplied me with more than a few pointers for online and local research. Paul continues to produce excellent works on local motoring and racing history.

The best purchase of all is a good spare-parts catalogue. These not only list every part, with superb exploded diagrams showing where absolutely every part goes, and in what order, they also list the designation of every clip, fastener and setscrew. Consequently, a 'grille to surround' setscrew may be obsolete, but the parts catalogue shows that it's part number YF7403. Cross-reference this to the guide in the catalogue, and it's a 'self tapper No8 x 3/4 pozi pan'. These are readily available online from hardware suppliers. Many mechanical parts are not unique to the Herald and were used in all sorts of cars back then, so think outside the box when tracking down obsolete parts which may be fitted to other models of the day, or have been remade by other owners' clubs. It can become addictive.

Enjoy your Herald, get out there and drive, and everywhere you go, you'll take a little piece of the 1960s with you, and if you want to take a little piece of Herald music with you, here's the perfect tune. Happy motoring!

For those of a musical bent, the music from the 1959 Herald release was available on vinyl. The photograph was taken at the Saxon Mill Restaurant near Stratford-upon-Avon, which is still in business today.